*Healing the Greatest Hurt*

*also from the authors*
*published by Paulist Press*

DELIVERANCE PRAYER
HEALING LIFE'S HURTS
HEALING OF MEMORIES
HEALING THE DYING (with Mary Jane Linn, C.S.J.)
PRAYER COURSE FOR HEALING LIFE'S HURTS
PRAYING WITH ANOTHER FOR HEALING

*Dennis Linn, S.J.*
*Matthew Linn, S.J.*
*Sheila Fabricant*

# Healing
# the Greatest Hurt

**Paulist Press**
New York/Mahwah

The Publisher gratefully acknowledges the use of "Thoughts on Praying for Departed 'Loved Ones' " by Douglas W. Schoeninger, Ph.D., from Vol. 6, No. 1 of *The Journal of Christian Healing*. Douglas Schoeninger, Ph.D. is Vice-President of the Institute for Christian Healing in Philadelphia, and Editor of *The Journal of Christian Healing*, in which this article was first published (Vol. 6, No. 1, 1984, 53–54). Dr. Schoeninger writes from his experience as a practicing clinical psychologist specializing in family therapy, and as a Deacon in the Presbyterian Church.

The Publisher also acknowledges Sheed and Ward for the use of an excerpt from *The Splendor of the Liturgy* by Maurice Zundel. Used by permission.

Photo credits: Carolyn Mohn, cover; Rick Smolan, p.2; Linn family, pp. 14, 81; Robert Beckhard, p. 22; Mia et Klaus, pp. 40, 142; John Murello, p. 58; Jerg Kroener, p. 74; Ed Lettau, p. 107

IMPRIMI POTEST:
Patrick J. Burns, S.J.
*Provincial, Wisconsin Province*
December 26, 1984

Library of Congress
Catalog Card Number: 85-60407

ISBN: 0-8091-2714-8

Published by Paulist Press
997 Macarthur Boulevard
Mahwah, N.J. 07430

Printed and bound in the United States of America

# Contents

This book is lovingly dedicated to

*Conrad Baars*
*Bill Carr*
*John Thomas Linn*
*Mary Jane Linn, C.S.J.*

**who pray for us**

# Chapter 1

# Healing Through Grieving

What is the greatest hurt that you have faced or might have to face? Several years ago during a retreat, seven people came to us with different problems, including homosexuality, chronic back pain and alcoholism. When we asked these seven people when their problems began, five of them told us that their problems began at the death of a close friend or family member. As these five people began in prayer to grieve and to heal the loss of their loved ones, their present problems began to disappear. Their problems in the present had been only symptoms of a greater hurt: the death of a loved one. When we lose what we most love, we can be most hurt.

The work of Dr. Thomas Holmes illustrates that the death of a loved one is the greatest hurt, resulting in a wide variety of physical, emotional, spiritual and social illnesses. Dr. Holmes had informants rank various stress situations and then constructed a stress scale.[1] The scale ranged from eleven stress points for a parking ticket, to seventy-five stress points for a divorce, and finally to the highest stress score of one hundred points for the death of a spouse. Dr. Holmes found that those who in any given year had more than three hundred stress points had a seventy percent chance of suffering ulcers, psychiatric disturbances, broken bones or other major health problems within the next two years, whereas those with less than two hundred points in a year had only a thirty-seven per-cent chance of illness. Based on their scores, Dr. Holmes even predicted accurately which football players would be injured during the next season.

All the situations Dr. Holmes ranked as the most destruc-tive involve losses: loss of a spouse through death or divorce, loss of physical health, loss of a job, etc. For many, the loss of a spouse through divorce or the loss of sight may be a greater hurt than the loss of a loved one through death. But we will follow Dr. Holmes in treating the loss of a loved one as the greatest hurt because it is the most common traumatic loss and illustrates the grief process present in all great hurts. Failure to work through this normal process of grieving can cause physical, emotional, spiritual and social illness.

The physical effects of unresolved grief are dramatically illustrated in Holmes' study by the death rate for widows during the first year following the death of their spouse. Such widows have ten times the normal death rate for married women the same age.[2] Men, after the loss of a spouse or a parent, also undergo a significant increase in death rate especially from accidents, heart disease and some infectious illnesses.[2a] Many cancer researchers have suggested that cancer typically develops six months to two years after a serious loss.[3] Recent studies at Mt. Sinai Hospital in New York help us understand the relationship between grief and physical illness. These studies found that after the death of a loved one, the immune system (especially the production of lymphocytes or white blood cells which fight infection and destroy cancer cells) is depressed for two months, leaving the bereaved person vulnerable to all illnesses, including cancer. As the survivors adequately grieve during the next four months, the immune system rebuilds itself back to near normal.[4] In a recent Institute of Medicine report on the effects of bereavement, twenty-one experts conclude that physical responses to grief may last six years or more because grief produces major changes in the respiratory, central nervous and hormonal systems and may substantially alter functions of the heart, blood and immune systems. The report also concludes that bereavement does less physical damage to women than men, in part because women more easily "cry on a friend's shoulder" to express and work through the grief.[5] Likewise, the recent research of Dr. James Pennebaker establishes that the bereaved who bear their pain alone have more physical ailments after a death, but those who work through their grief by confiding in another have no increase in health problems after a death.[6]

Not only on the physical level but also on the emotional level, many problems can be traced back to a loss which was not adequately grieved. From ten to twenty percent of new widows and widowers remain clinically depressed for a year or longer.[7] Dr. Erich Lindemann found that psychiatric patients had six times as many situations of loss requiring grieving in their lives as did the general population.[8] Another study found higher rates of divorce and crime among persons who had lost a parent during childhood.[9] The loss of a parent or sibling in childhood is especially hazardous for both short and long term mental health because instead of grieving after the death, children are more likely to grieve intermittently for years to come.[10] Unresolved grief damages teenagers emotionally too. In her study of unmarried teenage girls who had two or more pregnancies, Dr. Nancy Horowitz found that half of the girls had experienced a significant loss within three years prior to one of the pregnancies. The single most common loss was the death of a father. Dr. Horowitz believes that conceiving an illegitimate child may sometimes be a desperate effort to regain a lost loved one.[11] Among married couples who have lost a child, there is an extremely high incidence of marital difficulties and even divorce. For instance, seventy-five percent of married couples who have lost a child older than four years of age will experience divorce. Many counselors believe that this is because of the stress placed on a marriage when one partner is ready to grieve (usually the wife first) and the other isn't. Unresolved grief expresses itself in a wide variety of emotional difficulties, perhaps as many as there are ways of troubled behavior.

At the spiritual level, grief may bring us closer to God or drive us further away from God. When we (Matt and Dennis) worked as therapists at Wohl Psychiatric Clinic with depressed people, we would always ask them what triggered the depression. Clients would usually state that it began with a loss—of a husband, a child, a job, their own health, etc. As long as these patients clung to resentment toward themselves, others, and God because of the loss, they remained depressed and unable to work through their grief. During that same time we also gave retreats and we would ask retreatants a different question: "When were you closest to God?" To our surprise, our retreatants mentioned the same situations as our depressed clients— the loss of a husband, child, job, or their own health which had made them begin to pray and ask the Lord to fill their emptiness. One difference between these two groups was that our depressed clients had pushed God away because they were unable to grieve and forgive, while for our retreatants the experience of loss had drawn them closer to God because they knew their need for God and allowed him to love them in the midst of their grief.[11a]

When we cannot find a God of love in the midst of grief, the consequences can be very great at the social level. For example, the Ayatollah Khomeini's hatred for the Shah of Iran and for his American supporters began when Khomeini's own son was executed by the Shah. From Khomeini's unresolved grief came his desire for revenge which eventually caused an international crisis and embroiled the whole Middle East in war. In contrast to Khomeini, Daddy King's grief for his son led to peace rather than war. After Martin Luther King was murdered, Daddy King gathered the family and said that Martin's vision of peace would die along with Martin unless they each forgave the murderer. Together the family grieved for Martin. They wept until they could pray and forgive the murderer. Because of their process of grieving they have continued to this day to carry on Martin Luther King's vision of non-violent forgiving love.

Such healthy grieving leading to forgiving love has changed even places such as the notorious La Mesa Prison into a loving community. When Antonia Brenner experienced the death of her marriage through divorce, she chose to give others all the love she could no longer give her husband. She became a nun and went to live in the prison as Mother Antonia. She began reaching out to the prisoners, whom she calls "my sons." Mother Antonia teaches the prisoners to break the cycle of revenge by grieving for their loved one and forgiving the murderer. In the nine years since Mother Antonia began living in the prison, not one prisoner who has been released has taken revenge on the person who murdered his loved one.

Unresolved grief may underlie more social problems than we ordinarily think, and immobilize us from working for change. For example, when Michael Russell began working for the Brown Lung Association, he tried to organize millworkers to fight for legislation that would protect them from brown lung disease. He grew increasingly frustrated with the millworkers who, rather than planning concrete strategies for change, spent every meeting retelling stories of loved ones who had died and other ways their community had suffered from the disease. The turning point came when millworkers and organizers attended a meeting with government official Eula Bingham. As she entered the room, she began to cry with frustration over the congressional session she had just left. Soon everyone in the room was crying. When the crying ended, the millworkers were for the first time able to speak concretely and effectively for their cause. Eula Bingham's willingness to appear weak and vulnerable as she released her grief through tears gave the millworkers permission to release their grief for their deceased loved ones and their own continued suffering. At that meeting Michael Russell realized for the first time that his people had been paralyzed by corporate or "political" grief: "The resistance we find among poor people to organizing to free themselves from oppressive circumstances is the end effect of unresolved political grief."[12] Psychotherapist Joanna Macy believes that all of us are carrying more or less buried grief for political and social situations that destroy life, such as nuclear arms, world hunger and environmental pollution. After leading many "Despair Empowerment Workshops," she concludes that by facing our grief and despair and releasing our feelings we find new power to work for change.[13]

If grieving is so important, why don't we do it? Some of the blocks to grieving come from our culture, while others come from the situation surrounding the death itself. Often in our culture we are encouraged not to face grief but rather to deny our grief and "be strong." Our heroes and heroines are ordinarily not people like Eula Bingham who are willing to show weakness, but rather those who stand up straight and don't cry at funerals. One writer comments on the unintentional damage done by Jacqueline Kennedy's example at the funeral of her husband, President John Kennedy.[14] A generation of grieving American women felt that they should imitate Mrs. Kennedy, who remained publicly calm and in control at her husband's funeral. As Christians, we even tell bereaved family members that they should be happy their loved one has left to be with the Lord (or that Jesus loved the deceased so much that he took that person home). We forget that even Jesus grieved for his friend Lazarus (Jn 11:35–36). When we short-circuit the grieving process for even the noblest reasons, we inflict physical, emotional, spiritual and social destruction.

Sometimes the surrounding situation short-circuits the grieving process. Working through grief is more difficult when the death is sudden or traumatic, when there is much "unfinished business" with the deceased, or when the death aggravates unresolved grief over a previous loss. An example of the latter situation would be when the loss of a nurturing woman friend stirs up unhealed pain from the loss of our mother. Sometimes the unresolved grief may be for a wounded part of ourselves which was represented by our loved one, as when a man who was awkward as a boy grieves for the death of his football player son. This man grieves not only his son but also his own dreams of athletic ability that he hoped to finally fulfill through his son.[15]

Before we are healed, we may have to grieve many times not just for past losses but for present losses too. For example, a widowed person is not finished when grieving the loss of a spouse. Months later grief might resurface, but this time it is for loss of a parenting partner for rambunctious children, loss of physical intimacy, loss of a breadwinner as bills pile up, or loss of the listener who was the first to hear all exciting news. The more we love a person, the more aspects of his presence we are going to miss. Unless we grieve these losses we will be afraid to love and risk loss again. If we really miss someone, we can also congratulate ourselves on how deeply we have loved and on having the potential to love as deeply again.

If grieving is so important, how do we know if we are grieving? We may be very conscious of some of the symptoms of grief, such as when we are overwhelmed by loneliness on the anniversary of the death or when with tears we speak of a way that person was special to us. We may be less conscious that other symptoms are rooted in grief, such as emotional highs and lows, fatigue, loss of appetite, indecisiveness or in-ability to concentrate. Grieving and its accompanying symp-toms of separation anxiety are a normal process of working through loss, typically lasting six months to two years. But since grief is made of two alternating tendencies—one to avoid pain and the other to face painful reality—grief will oscillate between intense painful mourning and periods of avoidance of pain. We face or avoid the painful loss through a normal series of stages: shock and crying, hostility (at doctors, at being left with burdens), guilt (if only I . . . ), disturbance of activity (losing oneself in activity or the lethargy of loneliness and doing things alone), and finally acceptance of reality. But unresolved grief can become pathological grief, in which the symptoms of grief persist for years in low level form as "shadow grief" or in more severe symptoms such as those who sought help from us because of their homosexuality, chronic back pain and alcoholism.[16] Professional help is usually not needed for grief unless a person is stuck in the process and is either unable to face his painful feelings or is unable to resolve painful feelings such as stuck anger, guilt or depression. Other symptoms of stuck grief might be intense avoidance of reminders of the deceased, idealization of the deceased, prolonged grief with intense nightmares, and grief resulting in illness.[17] Normally, if we can share our feelings with another who has genuine empathy, we will move through the grief process.

How do we know if we have finished grieving or are just avoiding unresolved grief? When do we know we have grieved in a healthy way? Examples like Daddy King or Mother Antonia show us that the test for healthy grieving is to ask ourselves the question, "Am I more able to give and receive love with the deceased, God and others?" Can I receive love—through prayer, sacraments, taking time for fun, letting others hug me, take me out to dinner, or do for me some of the other special things my loved one may have done? Do I care for myself with proper food, exercise, sleep and activities that bring me life? Can I give love—letting my love for the deceased empower me to reach out to others as did Mary Magdalene or the disciples on the road to Emmaus? Can I let the deceased person join Jesus in interceding for me and in continuing to love me so that our relationship grows closer and more self-giving than ever? Am I getting closer to Jesus who, as he holds the deceased person in his heart wants to be with me in all the ways I miss my loved one?

If we haven't finished grieving, how can we heal our grief? What helps heal grief is to share all our feelings with a significant person who loves us unconditionally.[18] The person who can have empathy (feeling our feelings) rather than sympathy (feeling primarily his own feelings so he feels sorry for us and distances himself from our pain or gets overly involved in it) will help us move through grief. Sharing with others, especially those who have experienced similar loss (e.g., widows felt other widows were most helpful during their first year of bereavement),[19] is essential to moving through grief. But since most of the literature on grieving stresses sharing feelings with others and almost totally ignores the role of prayerfully sharing all with an empathetic, healing Jesus and of continuing to give and receive love with the deceased through prayer, this book will stress how to pray for the healing of grief. Because grief is primarily healed through friendship, sharing all with the greatest Friend brings another depth of healing. Through the heart of Jesus we can love and be loved by those we miss the most. Healing the greatest hurt with the greatest Friend unlocks the greatest love.

## Chapter 2

# Healing Grief for the One We Miss the Most

Spring 1948  John 7 mos.
          Denny 3

Mom 5 yrs.

At an early age, I (Matt) discovered the need to grieve and the destruction that happened if I didn't. When I was seven years old, my brother John, who was two, contracted bronchitis. I told my mother, "Don't worry. He just has a cold." But John died on the way to the hospital.

First, I went through the stage of denial, not believing that John was really dead. (Later, denial would take different forms, such as denying that I missed John or that I needed help.) But when I saw my parents come home with tears in their eyes, I knew I had lost my brother. And then I entered the second stage, of anger—anger against doctors who didn't help more or make house calls, anger against ambulance drivers who didn't drive faster to give the one more minute John needed, and even anger against John for leaving me. Years later I discovered that I also had anger against God who certainly could have given my brother another minute. Then I started to formulate bargains, such as I would forgive the doctor (who lived in our neighborhood) only if he would come and apologize or only if he would start making house calls again. I was in the midst of the five stages of grieving, based on the five stages of dying described by Elisabeth Kübler-Ross.[1]

### Five Stages of Grieving

| | |
|---|---|
| Denial: | I don't admit the loss. |
| Anger: | I blame others. |
| Bargaining: | I set up conditions before I am ready to forgive. |
| Depression: | I blame myself. |

Acceptance:   I accept the gifts passed on to me by my loved
              one and look forward to ongoing ways I can re-
              late with Jesus and the deceased.

Even though I moved in and out of the first three stages,
most of the time I found myself stuck in the fourth stage of
depression. In this stage the anger and blame shifts away from
others (e.g., God, doctors, the deceased) and onto myself. I began blaming myself for John's death. After all, I had told my
mother that John would be O.K. and perhaps delayed her in
getting the doctor. I also blamed myself for things left unsaid
and undone with John. If God took John, I thought, it must
be because I didn't take good care of him—and then I would
recall all our unreconciled quarrels. Finally, I blamed myself
for allowing John's death to hurt and destroy me. The more I
blamed myself, the more I lost all self-confidence and could not
even read properly in school. Later, in high school, I worked
very hard, but even when I got all "A's" I never felt good about
myself.

Finally I joined the Jesuits. I probably joined them because they had the longest training of any priests, and I figured
that I needed all the help I could get because I was such a mess.
Jesuit life began with a thirty-day retreat and a general confession in which I dumped all my sinfulness into the Father's lap.
I had ten pages of sins to confess in only fifteen minutes, so my
novice master told me to say just what was in my heart. I found
myself saying the one thing I hadn't written down and which
I had never faced before: "I feel responsible for the death of my
brother John. I don't feel that I loved him enough." And with
that I cried and couldn't go on because I had reached the point
of bringing before the Lord's love the part of myself I disliked
the most, the part that had never grieved and had never been
reconciled with my brother's death. My novice master smiled

and said that Jesus was rejoicing because he could forgive me a debt of five hundred rather than just fifty. I knew that was true. Suddenly Jesus' smile was within me, and as I forgave myself, I felt as though a huge concrete shell had burst open, giving me new freedom to be loved and to love rather than just to hate myself.

Forgiving myself brought me from the depression stage to the acceptance stage of grieving. Although breakthroughs occurred, most of my healing came gradually. During the following years, I came to be grateful for and use the many gifts that came from John's death. As a hospital chaplain I could be with parents who had lost a child because I knew what they felt and wanted to be sure they didn't continue feeling guilty. As a confessor, I was eager and able to lift the penitent's burden of guilt because I knew both the agony of feeling "I'm no good" and the power of Jesus' healing in confession. My suffering from events like John's death has moved me to pray for physical and inner healing when others are crippled and to even use the five stages of dying and grieving as a healing process. Not only has John's death gifted me to pray for healing of hurts but also to write seven books about it. Because I was so insecure as a child and adolescent, I wrote constantly to figure things out, to be exact, and to be sure I'd know what to say. This developed my gift of writing.

Best of all is my gift of Dennis, my brother, who is always by my side. I think the reason I'm close to Dennis is because when John died, I realized that I couldn't just take another brother for granted. I didn't want Dennis to die with fights unpatched or deep feelings unshared. My desire to have John and Dennis as brothers has also made it easy to relate to Jesus as brother—a brother who will never leave me and who rejoices to forgive five hundred rather than fifty. Jesus came with all these gifts when I was finally able to grieve John's death by forgiving God, others and myself until I could give and receive love.

Through prayer, especially each morning and night asking Jesus for John to channel God's love, I experience an ongoing relationship with John. I believe that even our Jesuit vocations are one way that John has channeled God's love to Dennis and myself. I have also sensed John's protecting presence many times. On one occasion I was caught in a small boat taking on water during a storm on treacherous Mobile Bay. In desperation, I asked John to intercede with Jesus, and the winds suddenly stopped as if a protective wall had surrounded us. Usually John's presence is not this dramatic but rather the quiet, peaceful bond of love I experience with my brother Dennis. And when I sit alone under a budding tree and feel like a brother to the universe, I know that John is sitting with me.

### Prayer For the Deceased One I Miss Most

Jesus, you wept over the death of Lazarus.
Show me my Lazarus, the one who brings the most
    tears to my eyes.
Show me my Bethany, the good times I miss.
Show me how you wept with Martha, Mary, and now
    with me.

Jesus, your love filled Lazarus with new life.
Show me my Lazarus breathing deeply your risen life.
Show me my Lazarus together with you, breathing your
    life into me.
Show me how each breath fills the empty places within
    myself.

Jesus, you asked us to unbind Lazarus.
Show me how I can unbind my Lazarus with
   forgiveness and love as deep as yours.
Show me how I am to let go and love others with this
   love.
And show me your dream to have us grow closer in
   your embrace now and forever.

## Chapter 3

# Love Is Stronger than Death

About a year ago, the three of us took turns praying with eight different people who were grieving for a deceased loved one. As we reflected together on our prayer sessions with these people, we saw that our expectations of what would help them most had changed. Before the prayer sessions, we thought that our role was to help each person find through Jesus' love the ability to "let go" of his or her loved one. But if the person had already begun to face the loss, what we found more important than letting go was to connect the grieving person with Jesus and the deceased. What was still needed from the deceased could then be received in a new relationship with the deceased loved one in Jesus. Once this new relationship began, the letting go of what the loved one had been for the grieving person in this life happened naturally.

For example, I (Sheila) prayed with fourteen year old Kim for the hurt of losing her beloved grandmother two years previously. Kim felt grief, guilt at ways she had failed to take care of her grandmother, and anger at relatives who hospitalized her grandmother. She was afraid to reach out and make new friendships because she feared she would lose them too. She spoke of "a big empty place" in her chest which "can never be filled up." Kim's longing for her past relationship with her grandmother was keeping her from living in the present. When Kim and I began our prayer by having Kim get in touch with all that she longed for, Kim recalled happy memories of times with her grandmother. As Kim's longing for her grandmother surfaced, I asked her to see Jesus with her grandmother. Kim saw Jesus inviting her to reach out and hold her grandmother. As she reached out, Kim experienced the joy of a reunion. I encouraged Kim to see herself in her grandmother's arms and remain there for several minutes, taking in all the love her grandmother still wished to give her. When Kim was ready, we prayed for her grandmother to be released more deeply into Jesus' love, and for Kim and her grandmother to continue to send love to each other through prayer. At the end of our prayer, Kim said that the painful empty place in her chest was filled up, with "lots of circulation." When we followed up with Kim three months later, she told us that she felt a new confidence that her relationship with her grandmother would never end and that this had freed her to reach out and make new friendships.

Healing grief over a loved one means not just healing a grieving person, but healing a relationship. The question Jesus asks is not so much "Are you willing to let go of your loved one?" as it is "How are the three of us going to be together now?" So long as Kim focused on the loss of her grandmother's physical presence, she was consumed with grief and unable to let go of their past relationship. When she focused on how through Jesus her grandmother continues to send love to her and allowed herself to take that in until she was filled, she was able to let go naturally of the past relationship and be healed of her grief. Kim had to let go of her grandmother's physical presence—not of her love.

Kim's deceased grandmother does not need physical presence because love transcends space and time. This was illustrated when we gave a retreat several years ago. Though many of those attending the retreat were divorced, seven were not only divorced but had not contacted their ex-spouses during the past five, ten or even fifteen years because they had no idea of where their ex-spouses lived. During the retreat these seven people prayed in various ways to forgive their ex-spouses. One year later we learned that in five of the seven cases, the ex-spouses had contacted them within a few weeks of being forgiven. Through the mystery of love that can transcend space and time, these ex-spouses knew without being told that they had been forgiven.

St. Paul tells us that love never ends (1 Cor 13:13), and our longing for our deceased loved ones is telling us a truth about the unendingness of love. When we deny or repress our longings for love by telling ourselves that we must "let go," our grief can become pathological.

Many people already feel connected to their deceased loved ones. In a cross-cultural study, Richard Kalish and David Reynolds found that forty percent of the people they studied had experienced a post-death encounter with a deceased loved one, and in almost all cases this was a positive and comforting experience which helped heal their grief.[1] In another cross-cultural study, J. Yamimoto compared mortality rates among widows in London, Boston and Tokyo. He found high death rates in all but the highly religious Japanese Buddhists who stressed ancestor worship. These widows sensed the presence of their husbands after death and suffered less grief.[2] In the United States, Fr. Andrew Greeley has found that fifty-one percent of widows and widowers experience contact with their deceased spouse, and that people who have such post-death encounters tend to be above average in emotional health, as compared to the general population.[3]

### Prayer for the Deceased and Spiritualism

Although Christianity may differ in its method from some of the traditions represented in cross-cultural studies (e.g., in its insistence that we not worship ancestors but rather celebrate the new relationship we have with the deceased through Jesus), Christian tradition has always had a place for our healthy desire to remain connected to our deceased loved ones. Christians praying the Apostles' Creed have affirmed for centuries their belief in the communion of saints, where living and dead communicate life to each other. Contemporary theologians such as Johannes Metz and Karl Rahner are calling Christians back to prayerfully participate in the communion of saints.[4]

Through prayer, Christians can remain forever connected to the deceased as love and forgiveness are passed back and forth (2 Cor 5:17–21; 1 Pet 4:6). Praying for the deceased in this way is not spiritualism (or spiritism). Spiritualism is rather the belief that spirits of the dead communicate with the living through a medium, which is forbidden in the Old Testament (Dt 18:10–14; Lv 19:31; 1 Chr 10:13–14). Each of these warnings focuses on a medium calling up the dead to consult the departed instead of consulting God. While forbidding even attendance at such séances, the Catholic Church encourages prayer for the deceased. Prayer for the deceased differs in three ways from the séance's "consulting" that Scripture forbids. First, there is no use of a medium but only prayer to Jesus Christ. Thus there is no giving up of one's identity to be controlled by another, but rather a conscious free relationship with Jesus. Second, there is no person calling up the spirits to be physically present, but rather we focus on Jesus first and then ask him to gather our departed loved ones however he chooses. Third, there is no replacing of the guidance of God by the guidance of the deceased, but only asking that the deceased be intercessors leading us deeper into God's guidance. There is no idolatry intimating that the deceased are more powerful or loving than God, but only reverence for the deceased as members of Jesus' body who can channel his infinite power and love. Today as in Old Testament times, spiritualism is attractive to grieving people until they discover how prayer can connect them in a healing way to their deceased loved ones. Spiritualism, like ancestor worship and every other heresy, is a distortion of a truth—the truth that love's power to connect us with the deceased never ends (1 Cor 13:13).[5]

## Old Testament Prayer for the Deceased

Many writers in the Old Testament emphasized the need for prayer which through love and forgiveness connects us to the deceased. Baruch prays that Yahweh will forgive and "remember not the misdeeds of our fathers" (Bar 3:1–8). Daniel too prays for God to forgive "our crimes and the crimes of our fathers . . ." (Dan 9:16ff). The Lord was so pleased with Daniel's prayer that he sent Gabriel with an answer of forgiveness for the present and past sins that had been confessed: "Seventy weeks are decreed for your people and for your holy city. Then transgression will stop and sin will end, guilt will be expiated, and everlasting justice will be introduced" (Dan 9:24). Finally, in 2 Maccabees 12:38–46 an offering is taken up to provide a sacrifice for the sins of dead soldiers who need God's forgiveness for having worn pagan amulets. Although Maccabees is contained only in the Greek or Septuagint version of the Old Testament (which was used by Paul in his Greek-speaking churches), the practice of praying for the dead was widely accepted.[5a] The promptness in praying for the sinful soldiers, the generous collection given by the whole army, and the presumption that the Jerusalem priests would accept this collection indicate that this was not an innovation but an accepted Jewish practice.

The Maccabean custom of praying for the dead was praised as "excellent and noble" (2 Mac 12:43) and continued as part of the official Jewish sabbath service at the time of Jesus.[6] Many Jews thought that *gehenna* (which was their place of punishment after death, later translated as hell) could be a place of temporary suffering. Even condemned souls in gehenna could gain freedom from their suffering as the living recited Jewish prayers such as the Shema.[7] This custom is still reflected in modern Jewish worship. The closing prayer at the end of every synagogue service is the Kaddish, and it is cus-

tomary for all those who are mourning to pray this ancient
prayer for their deceased loved ones. The Kaddish is also
prayed on the *jahrzeit* or yearly anniversary of the death. Another Jewish tradition is for a family to pray the ancient *Yizkor*
in the synagogue four times a year for the departed and make
a charitable offering. (See Appendix B, Part III for an excerpt
from the *Yizkor*.) This charitable sacrifice for the dead can be
traced back to ancient Talmudic times.[8] Perhaps this ancient
Jewish tradition of prayer for the deceased is why Jesus was so
at home praying for his deceased friend Lazarus or for Jairus'
daughter.

　　Not only did ancient Jewish tradition include the living
praying for the deceased, but it also asked the deceased to pray
for the living.

> The practice of praying for the intercession of the
> dead is of early origin. Caleb on reaching Hebron vis-
> ited the cave of Machpelah, and prayed to the patri-
> arch to be saved from cooperating in the conspiracy
> of the scouts sent by Moses to make a report of the
> conditions in the Holy Land (Sotah 34b). The Tal-
> mud mentions visiting the cemetery to request the
> dead to pray for the living (To'an 16a).[9]

Thus at the time of Jesus there is growing rabbinical support
for the doctrine of the communion of saints where living and
dead prayerfully help each other.

　　Although "communion of saints" is a Christian term, the
concept is rooted in the Hebrew idea of corporate personality.
The idea of corporate personality meant that the Hebrew social
group included deceased ancestors and the unborn as well as
presently living members. Each member of the group shared
so fully in the psychic life of all members that each could rep-
resent the corporate personality of the entire group.[9a]

## Early Christian Prayer for the Deceased

The tradition of prayer for the deceased did not stop with the time of Jesus but continued into the New Testament period, especially in the Greek-speaking churches. Just as Paul (or whoever wrote the letters to Timothy) believed that prayers help the living through Jesus' intercession (1 Tim 2:1–4), that author also believed that prayers could help the deceased Onesiphorus through Jesus' intercession (2 Tim 1:18). Paul's Corinthian Church even followed a mysterious practice of using the prayers of baptism to help the dead (1 Cor 15:29) which Paul does not condemn as heresy even in this letter searching for practices to condemn. He mentions this almost casually and thus gives tacit approval to the Corinthian practice of praying for the deceased. Paul can pray for the deceased because he believes that through baptism we become members of the mystical body of Christ (1 Cor 12), relating in a love that never ends (1 Cor 13) and is stronger than death (Rom 8:38). Our unity in this body of Christ is so powerful that it wipes away distinctions between Jew and Greek, male and female, slave and free until we are one in Christ Jesus (Gal 3:27–28). If one member of the body suffers, the healthy members come to the aid of the weak (1 Cor 12:26). If we could not through Jesus relate in prayer to the dead, then we would be saying that Jesus had two unrelated, separate bodies rather than the one, undivided body that Scripture proclaims. The early Christians realized that this unity lasted beyond death and bound the living and the dead (1 Cor 15) into the "communion of saints" who could help each other as do two hands because they were all members of Jesus' body.

Those writing the New Testament taught their earliest followers to pray for the dead. During persecution these early Christians hid in the catacombs to pray. There they buried their dead and carved on their tombs requests for prayer. For example, on one catacomb tombstone now in the Lateran Museum the husband declared that he set the inscription for his wife Lucifera "in order that all brethren who read it may pray for her, that she may reach God."[10] Similarly, outside Rome in 180 A.D. the epitaph of Abercius, bishop of Hieropolis in Phrygia, requests prayer.[11] Other second and third century inscriptions ask for peace and refreshment or for admission amongst the saints. One expert describes how the accompanying pictures even relate to praying for the dead.

> The faithful prayed for the dead, entreating God to protect their souls, as he protected Daniel in the lion's den, the three young men in the furnace, Noah in the ark, and Susanna against the two elders. With the same intention and in order to invite the visitors of these subterranean cemeteries to pray for the dead, these biblical figures were depicted near the sepulchres—Daniel and Noah in the hypogeum of the Flavii as early as the first century, and all four together at the beginning of the second century in the Capella Greca.[12]

Thus St. Paul and other Christians "as early as the first century" prayed for their dead. Such prayers found their roots not just in the practice of Jesus but also in the teaching of Jesus' apostles, especially as more were martyred and the expected second coming didn't come to reunite living and dead. In the East John Chrysostum and in the West Cyprian (245 A.D.) each regarded the practice of praying for the dead as emanating from the apostles' teachings.[13] Jungmann in *Mass of the Roman Rite* agrees and traces how memorial Eucharists for the dead have roots as ancient as the pre-Christian graveside memorial meal (*refrigerium*) and sacrifices. Early Eucharists, such as that reported in the Apocryphal Acts of St. John (170 A.D.) were often conducted at the grave on the third day after burial or a year later as occurred with the annual memorial Mass in Smyrna for Polycarp (155 A.D.). By the third century praying for the deceased on their memorial day was so customary that Tertullian writes:

> The faithful wife will pray for the soul of her deceased husband, particularly on the anniversary of his falling asleep. And if she fails to do so, she has repudiated her husband as far as in her lies.[14]

Tertullian even advises a widower not to marry again because he would find himself in the embarrassing position of still praying for his first wife.

The importance of praying for the dead is taught by many of the early Fathers such as Tertullian, Origen, Ephrem, Cyprian, Ambrose, Augustine, Basil, Gregory of Nyssa, Gregory of Nanzianzus, Bede and Gregory the Great.[15] Praying for the dead was not just a private practice of saints, for in 337 A.D. Emperor Constantine died and his body was placed before the altar while priests and people prayed for his soul.[16] By the fourth century commemoration Eucharists were held, especially on the third, seventh, ninth, thirtieth, and fortieth days after a person's death.[17] Two centuries later, priests were celebrating the Eucharist for the dead not just episodically but on a series of consecutive days ranging from three to forty days. Unfortunately, this holy rite deteriorated by the Middle Ages into a magical practice which promised unfailing results from the repetition of a set number of hurried Masses. The reformers rightly rejected this magical abuse, but in rejecting the Eucharist for the deceased, they rejected a deep Christian tradition.

## Prayer for the Deceased and Purgatory

The early Christians in both East and West set great store by the accounts of the saints who helped the dead by their prayers. For example, St. Perpetua (who died in 203 A.D.) was imprisoned when her dead and unbaptized brother Dinocrates appeared to her in a vision. He seemed to be wounded, pale, thirsty and unable to drink from a fountain. After she prayed daily for him to be taken into heaven, she was rewarded with another vision of him happy, healed and able to drink from the eternal fountain.[18] Roman Catholics continue to believe that there is an intermediate stage of purification (purgatory) between death and the perfect love we need to give and receive in heaven (1 Cor 3:10–15; Mt 5:26; Jn 14:2; Lk 12:48; Rev 21:27). Saints such as Teresa of Avila, Catherine of Bologna, and the Curé d'Ars were revered for their devotion in praying for the souls in purgatory.[19] The Curé d'Ars gave one explanation of why so much healing comes to the living as they pray for the deceased: "We must pray for them so that they will pray much for us." The Council of Trent (Session XXV, Dec. 4, 1569) stated that the prayer of the faithful, especially the Eucharist, helps the souls of the deceased. The Council of Vienna (1858) added that those in purgatory can intercede for us, as many saints believed.[20] Pope Leo XIII later attached an indulgence to a prayer invoking the souls in purgatory.[21] Thus especially during November and on All Souls Day (Nov. 2) Roman Catholics continue the saints' practice of praying for the dead to be loved and forgiven. This tradition of helping our fellow departed pilgrims through Eucharist, alms, prayer and a loving life was recently reaffirmed in Vatican II's document *Lumen Gentium*.[22]

Roman Catholic tradition is also evolving in its view of purgatory. At one time Catholics saw purgatory as a fire-filled prison run by a harsh God who demanded payment for our sins. This image of a harsh, punitive God was reflected in the sacrament of reconciliation where sins were judged, forgiven and given a fitting penance. Since Vatican II, this sacrament emphasizes healing rather than the juridical dimension of payment for sin. The face-to-face encounter with the priest and the touch of his hand in absolution are signs of belief in a loving, healing God rather than a distant, judgmental one. Similarly, our modern understanding of the state we call purgatory is not a prison but rather a hospital where the deceased who were hurt in this life grow in the ability to receive all the healing love God wishes to give them (Heb 12:23). Thus dogmatic theologian Fr. Richard McBrien suggests that the suffering of purgatory does not involve external punishment such as scorching flames. Rather the suffering is the intrinsic pain we feel in surrendering our self-centeredness so that God might grow within us.

> Purgatory is best understood as a process by which we are purged of our residual selfishness so that we can really become one with the God who is totally oriented to others. . . . The kind of suffering associated with purgatory, therefore, is not suffering inflicted upon us from outside as a punishment for sin, but the intrinsic pain that we feel when we are asked to surrender our ego-centered self so that the God-centered loving self may take its place. It is part of the process by which we are called to die and rise with Christ.[22a]

Thus according to McBrien's view, supported centuries ago by St. Catherine of Genoa, we pray for the deceased not because we want to convince God to receive them into heaven but so that our love will empower them to open up more to God's healing love.[23] We pray to open them to receive healing love from a God who wishes them to hear: "This day you will be with me in paradise" (Lk 23:43). If they are already with God in paradise, our prayers draw them deeper into the love of Jesus offered through our hearts.

Jesus compared our transition from this world into paradise by saying that we must be born again (Jn 3:3). A newborn child is often frightened and crying even though it is surrounded by love and care. As the mother holds and strokes the baby, it gradually begins to rest in her love. When we die, we like the baby will be unable to receive all the love that awaits us. Each of us will die with unhealed hurts needing healing love from the members of Jesus' body. Those who loved us here and who drew us into the heart of Jesus continue to offer their deeper love to help us grow in giving and receiving love, just as a mother who loved and nourished her baby in the womb can continue to love it after birth. As we grow in love, we can also return more love to the living who remain so special to us. Love between living and deceased is like therapy, healing this life's self-centeredness and deepening our capacity to dwell together in God who is love (1 Jn 4:16).

Support for a state in which some of the deceased need the prayers of the living to grow in giving and receiving love comes from contemporary research with resuscitated patients who have had "near death experiences." Dr. Raymond Moody's research supports the view that there seems to be a period of adjustment after death for learning and receiving correction. Some of these patients report seeing a "realm of bewildered spirits" in which the dead are trapped and trying to communicate with their living relatives in the hope of moving on to heaven.[24] Since there is no time in eternity, this may be the stage when the prayers of the living are used by Jesus Christ to teach a deceased person how to give and receive love.

### Prayer for the Deceased and Other Traditions

Many other traditions find it helpful to pray for the deceased. In the East John Chrysostom stated: "When that awe-inspiring sacrifice lies displayed on the altar, how shall we not prevail with God by our entreaties for the dead?"[25] Egypt's oldest formulary, the Serapion, has a prayer for the deceased: "Sanctify all who have died in the Lord and number them among your holy troops and give them peace and dwelling in thy kingdom."[26] The Orthodox Church today believes in the power of prayer to even help those in hell as well as those more healed souls being judged at twenty-two telonia (celestial toll houses where the soul is rigorously examined on a particular sin).[27] Though the Roman Catholic Church does see hell as a permanent and not as a temporary state, it encourages us to pray for everyone since we cannot be sure whether anyone has chosen or ever will choose hell, the state of eternally refusing Jesus' love.

Besides the Orthodox, Protestants are rediscovering praying for the dead (see Appendix B). Some Methodists are returning to the tradition of John Wesley who in 1752 based praying for the faithful departed on "thy kingdom come" of the Lord's Prayer.

> In this kind of general prayer, therefore, "for the faithful departed," I conceive myself to be clearly justified, both by the earliest antiquity, by the Church of England, and by the Lord's Prayer; although the Papists have corrupted this spiritual practice into praying for those who die in their sins.[28]

Similarly, in replying to a writer who had attacked various practices as second century corruptions, Wesley observed:

Praying thus for the dead "that God would shortly accomplish the number of his elect and hasten his kingdom" and anointing the sick with oil, you will not easily prove to be any corruptions at all.[29]

John Wesley had been immersed in the Anglican tradition which today is rediscovering that prayer for the deceased is as traditional as *The Book of Common Prayer*.[30] A group of Anglican theologians reporting to the Archbishops' Commission on Christian Doctrine write of how the living may usefully pray for the dead, through Jesus Christ, that during the state of purification they may develop "a deepening of character and a greater maturity of personality."[31] In England nearly every Anglican bishop has appointed a priest to offer the Eucharist for the deceased as recommended by Anglican psychiatrist Dr. Kenneth McAll in *Healing the Family Tree*.[32] An Anglican minister told him: "For centuries people have celebrated funerals, usually some days after the person has died. If we can pray for a person three days after their death, surely we can continue to pray for them."

Remarkable healing happens as other churches rediscover the power of the Eucharist for the deceased. For example an Episcopal church in Texas asks each day for the Lord to give them names of the deceased that Jesus wants prayed for at the Eucharist. One day they received a name that no one knew, until later that day a man visited the curate. He said he had quit the church after murdering someone and that morning at home had been led to return. The pastor asked whom he had murdered, and the man gave the name of the stranger they had prayed for that morning.

But besides pastors, many Protestant therapists are helping their clients pray for deceased family members because it is therapeutically healthy. Dr. Carl Jung believed that mourners should not build huge funeral monuments but should rather pray for the dead as Catholics did at the Eucharist.[33] With a similar belief, Dr. Kenneth McAll for the past twenty years has helped thousands who were not helped by normal psychiatric methods. He and Dr. William Wilson of Duke University find that prayer and especially the Eucharist for the deceased is particularly helpful for treating stubborn illness such as anorexia nervosa where the victim starves herself almost as if trying to join the deceased. Using this approach as a key, Dr. McAll has treated two hundred and five anorexics with eighty-six percent success, and Dr. Wilson has treated twelve anorexics with one hundred percent success.[34] Others such as Presbyterian deacon and family therapist Dr. Douglas Schoeninger and his Baptist colleague Frances Bailey find that praying for the deceased is one of the best ways to resolve grief and inherited family conflicts (cf. Appendix B). Today as at Bethany, Jesus weeps for the deceased and then looks at us and says: "Unbind him and let him go free" (Jn 11:44).

But what if, despite the centuries of tradition, we still doubt whether our loving prayers can help the departed? What if our doubt is so deep that we ever wonder if there is even life after death?

In Dostoevsky's classic *The Brothers Karamozov*, a woman confronts the famous holy monk, Fr. Zossima, and asks for help to regain her belief in life after death. Will there be life after death or just burdock weeds growing on her grave? Why as a child is it so easy and as an adult so difficult to believe in life beyond the grave? What proof can overcome her fear that life disappears without a trace? The wise Fr. Zossima answers her:

There's no proving it, though you can be convinced of it.

How?

By the experience of active love. Strive to love your
neighbor actively and indefatigably. In as far as you
advance in love you will grow surer of the reality of
God and of the immortality of your soul. If you attain
to perfect self-forgetfulness in the love of your neighbor, then you will believe without doubt, and no
doubt can possibly enter your soul. This has been
tried. This is certain. [35]

The more we enter into the deepest love, the more we will
know that love lasts forever in the communion of saints.

*Chapter 4*

# How To Pray for the Deceased*

*This chapter is available in condensed form as a leaflet entitled "Prayer for the Dead that Heals the Living." See pages 243 and 245.

The masterpiece film "Gandhi" portrays the bloody civil war following the partition of India into Moslem Pakistan and Hindu India. Deaths brought only retaliation and more deaths until Gandhi, himself a Hindu, began a fast and vowed not to eat until the killing ended, even if it meant his own death. A crazed Hindu visited the fasting Gandhi and threw a piece of bread at him while screaming: "I am already going to hell and I don't want your death on my soul too." Gandhi replied: "Why are you going to hell?" The Hindu shook as he answered: "I had a small boy who was killed by the Moslems, and so I took the first Moslem child I could find and killed it by smashing its head against a wall." Gandhi with hope in his eyes said: "I know a way out of hell. Many boys are now left without parents because of the killings. Find a Moslem boy the same age as your son and adopt him. Only be sure you raise him as a Moslem." The wildness left the Hindu's eyes as he began to sob and finally collapsed on Gandhi's bed. Gandhi put his hand on the Hindu's head and the man received it like absolution. When the Hindu left he had peace in his heart. He had chosen forgiveness for himself and his country rather than choosing revenge. A week later all Hindus went to their temples and Moslems to their mosques to pledge that they would forgive and stop the vengeful killing. Grief was turned to forgiveness and India had peace overnight.

Often as in Gandhi's India, the healing of grief is not only very difficult but also the key to personal and social peace. How can we heal grief? In the raising of Lazarus (Jn 11) Jesus gives us a model with three steps:

(1)  share our heart with Jesus (Jn 11:1–41);
(2)  unbind and heal the deceased (Jn 11:44);
(3)  give thanks for new life (Jn 11:42).


### First Step: Share Our Heart with Jesus

When our friend Bill died of bone cancer after three years of suffering, I did not feel anger at God but rather relief that Bill had finally died. It was not until a month after Bill's death that I got in touch with my anger, which helps to pinpoint the wound needing healing. At that time I went to visit another friend who was dying of bone cancer. He, like Bill, was a counselor now sidelined from helping hurting people. I looked at his emaciated body and heard in my heart an angry voice scream, "Where are you, God? Why are our prayers so useless?"

In my prayer that evening, I told Jesus all the things that made me angry about Bill's death. "Why did you let it happen that way? Why bones collapsing into jelly? Why pain that only constant morphine could touch? Why the final moments of choking and a tortured body? And worst of all, why in the last moments Bill's waves of anger that beat against even those he loved most?"

After I had gotten all my anger out, I went to the cross where I heard Jesus choking, writhing in pain and dying the same kind of death as Bill. In fact I heard Jesus shouting just as I had about the unfairness of death, "My God, my God, why have you forsaken me?" I saw how Jesus' most painful moment didn't distance the Father but only drew him closer. Then I could go back and watch Bill's painful death and see it not distancing the Father but drawing the Father closer to his Son suffering in Bill. I knew that the Father had responded to

Bill's ugly death just as I did. The Father is at least as loving as I am, and the ugliness of Bill's death had only made me love Bill more and have a greater longing to be with him and comfort him.

What I discovered as I prayed was that I was angry at Bill's death because it was perhaps the kind of death I feared most. In his final moments, Bill's morphine ceased to work and he found himself trapped in delirium and fighting off those he loved most. My deepest fear was that I, like Bill, would die aware only of pain and not of God's love or the love of others in the room. If I could love Bill regardless of what he said or did at his death, then I could trust the Father to be there for me at my death even if I tried to push him away. So I asked the Father to heal in me anything that kept me from trusting that he would be there for me when I died at my worst. Then I breathed into Bill the Father's love to heal the abandonment that Bill, like Jesus, must have felt at his death. Then I breathed in from Jesus, the Father and Bill all I wanted them to be for me at the hour of my death. I was finally healing what a month before I felt was finished.

In the first step of sharing our heart with Jesus, we tell Jesus whatever we are feeling, especially our negative feelings that could block our relationship with him. Often anger at God masquerades as a distaste for prayer or inability to feel his love. Perhaps we feel angry like the Jews at Lazarus' tomb questioning, "He opened the eyes of the blind men. Could he not have prevented this man's death?" (Jn 11:39). Or perhaps, like Martha and Mary, we may feel Jesus deserted us and insist, "Lord, if you had been here my brother would never have died" (or never died such a painful death). In this step we, like Martha and Mary, may need to forgive Jesus until he becomes not someone who sends a painful and untimely death nor someone who was absent and uncaring, but rather as Martha and Mary and the Jews finally experienced him. They saw Jesus with tears in his eyes and said, "See how much he loved Lazarus" (Jn 11:36).

In the step of sharing our heart with Jesus, you may find the following way of praying helpful.

• Join Jesus as he loves Martha and Mary and all those who weep for Lazarus.

• Ask Jesus to help you recall a time when a loved one died.

• Gratefully recall the good times you had with your loved one. Tell Jesus all the ways you miss that person and let any tears flow. Face all the loss.

• With Martha and Mary, forgive Jesus for any way you feel that he wasn't there, and allow Jesus to be with you in any way you need him now.

• Let Jesus continue to love you and grieve with you for your deceased loved one.


### Second Step: Unbind and Heal the Deceased

Shortly before Bill died, I invited him to join us in giving a five-day workshop on "Healing the Greatest Hurt." During the workshop I especially looked forward to breakfast each morning because I always awoke with something I wanted to ask or say to Bill before he died. So, for example, we spent one breakfast asking forgiveness of each other. I asked forgiveness for such things as the pain I caused him by not being ecumenical enough and by not inviting him to share the gifts of his Episcopalian tradition. Bill asked forgiveness for being so serious with me and not calling forth my gift of play. (Perhaps that is why he made sure that my last memory of him would be flying a model airplane he bought.) I spent another breakfast telling Bill how he had gifted me and what I would always treasure about him. Bill responded by telling me what I meant to him. By the final breakfast I felt as though I had nothing else I needed to say or do with him except to ask about his funeral. So I asked him what he would like me to do when I received word of his death. Bill told me not to come to Philadelphia for his funeral but rather to celebrate with some of his other friends near my home in Omaha who would be unable to travel so far. Then Bill suggested several things I might do with his family after he died.

After that last breakfast, Bill helped us relive our childhoods as we put together two wooden model airplanes he had bought. I am so glad that my final memory of Bill was flying those airplanes with him. To me our two airplanes and their free flight through the air were a symbol of our days together. Like the planes, I felt such a freedom in having given Bill everything I had and in receiving everything he could give me. I felt as though our two spirits were indeed flying together. We had unbound one another and set each other free.

Perhaps when I visit Bill's home later this month I will think of things that I still wish I had said or done with Bill. If so, I can become connected with Bill and Jesus in prayer and we can again do what we did each morning at breakfast. In praying for a loved one, I find the following ways of prayer helpful in carrying out the same invitation that Jesus gave concerning his loved one Lazarus. "Unbind him," Jesus told Lazarus' friends, "and let him go free" (Jn 11:44).

• Ask Jesus to help you remember a deceased person whom you need to unbind by being reconciled with him or her.

- Tell Jesus and the deceased person what you wish you had said and done. "If only I had . . ."

- Look at how much Jesus loves and wants to heal both you and the deceased person. As you move into the depths of his healing love, see if Jesus says or does anything for you or leads the deceased person to do what will bring love and forgiveness to you and closeness to Jesus.

- Let Jesus hug both of you. As you get filled with life, breathe it out upon the deceased person. Let Jesus tell you how he wants you to continue to love each other in ways that bring the three of you closer forever. Then join the deceased person in breathing out Jesus' healing love toward those whom either of you have been hurt by or have hurt, so that neither of you is bound by any unhealed relationships.

### Third Step: Give Thanks for New Life

When I first received news of Bill's death, I did not feel anger at God but rather relief that Bill was no longer in pain and that Jesus had welcomed Bill home. So I skipped the first two steps in healing grief and started with step three, giving thanks. We can go through the steps outlined in this chapter in any order, and sometimes we can be going through two or three of the steps at the same time. In grieving for Lazarus, the one Jesus missed most, the steps Jesus took were simply ways of sharing his heart and not rigid rules. Our prayer can be healing when we simply share with Jesus what is in our heart and let him share his heart with us.

So, in Jesus' presence, I started by giving thanks to Bill for all he had meant to me. Much of it was like the breakfast conversation with Bill, but I found myself adding a few new things. For example, since being with Bill, two of my friends had moved. Instead of just saying goodbye to them, I took time to do with them what I had done with Bill. So I gave thanks to Bill for the way he had taught me to say goodbye to people, to not wait until tomorrow to say and do those things which a person needs to receive today. Bill has given me the gift of living more in the present moment and not taking others or tomorrow for granted.

During the past year my prayer of thanks has changed as I continue to see new ways that Bill has given me life. Last month I gave thanks when returning from war-torn Guatemala, because for the first time in a war-torn country I had felt no fear of death. Today I thanked Bill that I could visit my friend with bone cancer and not feel anger at God but rather God's compassion.

But most of all I am thankful for my ongoing relationship with Bill. Even now, when I get stuck in writing this book, I listen to a tape of Bill's songs and picture him singing them again for me at the side of Jesus while I breathe in the love of both of them united together. Receiving Bill's and Jesus' love allows me to get "unstuck" and I am able to take the next loving step in writing this book. Before his death, when this book was still in the dreaming stage, the three of us shared our dreams with Bill. Now that Bill knows the answers from the other side of death, I count on him to intercede for our writing, believing that he will want to continue to love us and future generations after death in many of the same ways he did before death.

Thus the third step of giving thanks celebrates our ongoing relationship with Jesus and the deceased. We celebrate all the ways in which that relationship helps us to receive love so that we may love God and others more. When grieving for his beloved friend Lazarus, Jesus gave thanks for how Lazarus' death was one more opportunity to experience the Father's care. With Jesus we pray, "Father, I thank you for having heard me." (Jn 11:41).

• Thank the Lord for any ways your loved one's death has given you new life (e.g., a deeper prayer life, no longer taking people for granted, reaching out to make new friends, getting involved in new activities, a sense of that person's intercession for you, caring for those he or she left behind, etc.).

### Simplifying Prayer

The three steps of healing our relationship with Jesus, healing our relationship with the deceased, and then giving thanks may seem difficult immediately after the death of a loved one. It may be difficult to pray because we may have anger against God or fear that if we get close to him, God too will leave us as did our loved one. As physical and emotional exhaustion shut down the imagination, we may grope in one-way conversations with a seemingly silent God. We do not have to see, hear, or feel anything in prayer but only know that our longing for our deceased friend is also a longing for our deepest Friend. We can simply say "Jesus" and breathe him into ourself and into the one we miss most.

Or our prayer may be a simple conversation, like that between one wise mother and her child. Five year old Mike had found his baby brother dead in his crib one morning. Mike loved his roommate brother and was heartbroken. Two years later Mike was refusing to go to school. Since he was doing well in school and had many friends, Mike's mother knew that there must be something else bothering him. She was led to take Mike back to the scene of his brother's death.

"Mike, can you see your bedroom and Jesus in the corner?"

"Yes."

"Let Jesus take you over to the crib and show you Tom the morning you found him dead. What is Jesus saying and doing?"

"Jesus has his hand on my shoulder and he is sad. He says Tom died not because of anything I did but because he wasn't made right."

"Do you fear that I too might die or get hurt if you go to school?"

"Yes."

"What does Jesus say?"

"He says he will never leave me."

From that day on, Mike went to school with no fear. Sometimes we, like Mike, are children frightened of death who need simple words of reassurance from Jesus.

### Unbinding and Healing the Deceased at the Eucharist

The most difficult step in healing grief is usually step two, healing the relationship with the deceased. One of the most powerful ways to heal our relationship with a deceased person is the way the grieving Emmaus disciples were healed—by recognizing Jesus in the breaking of the bread (Lk 24:30–35). When Jesus joined the disciples on the road to Emmaus, they began to pour out their grieving hearts to him and take on his reconciling heart. But it was the becoming one with the reconciling Jesus at the breaking of the bread that healed their grief to the point where they could return back to normal life. When we, like the disciples, become one with the reconciling Jesus at the Eucharist, our grief too can be healed.

During one of our retreats, we held a Eucharist for forgiving one person. One of the participants was Bob, a priest whose family and friends had been killed by Adolf Hitler. Bob had plotted to kill Hitler, but was captured and imprisoned. Only the end of the war prevented Hitler from killing Bob. Although Hitler had been dead for thirty-five years by the time of the retreat, Bob still could not bury him. He could neither forgive Hitler nor pray for him. Bob was stuck in unresolved grief. It may sound strange to speak of Bob grieving for Hitler, but unresolved grief for a deceased person is simply unfinished business with that person, and until the living person can forgive himself and the deceased, the living one will continue to grieve.

When we asked everyone at the Eucharist to think of one person that each needed to forgive, Bob immediately thought of Hitler. Then we asked each person to exchange one shoe with another person, as a sign of trying to walk in the shoes of the person being forgiven. When Bob handed one of his shoes to the person on his left, he was surprised to receive in exchange a soldier's boot—just like Hitler's boot. When Bob tried to compassionately imagine what it was like to walk in Hitler's shoes, he became stuck. Bob was so enraged by Hitler's hardness of heart that he could feel no compassion for the hurts in Hitler's life, although he tried to imagine them. How could a man be so hard-hearted as to kill millions of Jews? If only Hitler had repented and changed, Bob thought, he could be forgiven.

But then Bob saw that in his very inability to forgive unconditionally, he was just like Hitler. For thirty-five years he had hard-heartedly refused to forgive Hitler's hard-heartedness. Bob felt like a hypocrite as he recalled his seminary education where he had had more opportunities than Hitler to learn about forgiveness. Bob's anger was now turned upon himself, until he saw how Jesus had forgiven him and used him as a priest despite his hard-hearted attitude toward Hitler. As Bob accepted Jesus' forgiveness, he was able to forgive and pray for Hitler during the rest of the Eucharist. After the Eucharist, Bob realized that he was free of back pain for the first time in thirty-five years. In completing his unfinished business with Hitler, Bob had literally taken Hitler off his back and finally buried him.

At the Eucharist Bob did the four steps Jesus gives us for forgiving:

> *Love* your enemies, *do good* to those who hate you, *bless* those who curse you, and *pray* for those who persecute you (Lk 6:27–28).

Bob's forgiveness began with the decision to *love* Hitler even if he hadn't felt like loving for thirty-five years. Second, Bob did a loving action—he put on another's shoe as a sign of wanting to enter Hitler's world. The second step is to *do good* to the person who hurt us or to someone like that person. Third, Bob tried to change his own thinking about Hitler. Bob tried to enter Hitler's world and imagine how Hitler had suffered so that he could think and feel like Hitler rather than continuing to judge what he didn't understand. Bob was trying to find the good in Hitler so that he could *bless* him. The word bless comes from the Latin *benedicere*, meaning "to say good things." As he entered Hitler's world, Bob could not find much good, but he *could* say, "I am just like Hitler, and Jesus forgives and blesses both of us." Bob had stopped judging and started forgiving. During the rest of the Eucharist Bob took the fourth step as he joined Jesus in *praying* for Hitler to be forgiven and healed. As Bob kept saying with Jesus, "Father, forgive him, for he knows not what he is doing," Bob's forgiveness deepened into Jesus' unconditional forgiving love. The gift of Jesus' forgiveness is usually given whenever his steps to forgiveness are taken.

If you, like Bob, wish to heal your relationship with a deceased person by becoming one with Jesus at the Eucharist, following are suggestions for letting each part of the liturgy become a way of extending love and forgiveness to the deceased. You may wish to begin by writing down the name of the person for whom you are going to pray. If possible, place the paper on the altar (if it is a special Eucharist for the dead) or hold it in your hands throughout an ordinary Eucharist.

*Sign of the Cross:* Make the sign of the cross invoking the power of Jesus' cross to deliver living and dead from all evil (Col 11:19–21).

*Penance Rite:* Pray for *forgiveness.* Ask forgiveness for any ways in which you and others hurt the deceased person. Ask Jesus to show you any attitudes or behaviors you have criticized in the deceased that are also a part of you, and ask Jesus' forgiveness just as Bob asked forgiveness for hard-heartedly judging Hitler's hard-heartedness. Then with Jesus forgive that person for the ways you and others may have been hurt by him or her. Ask Jesus to show you how he wants to ask his Father to heal and love the deceased person during this Eucharist.

*Offertory:* Offer the gift of the deceased person to the Father and thank the Father for all the good that has come to you and others because of the deceased person. Perhaps what you will see are the ways the deceased's very woundedness has brought forth great mercy and forgiveness, as Hitler's woundedness brought forth mercy and forgiveness in Bob. Whether you can find much or little goodness in the deceased, let the Father bless that goodness and all the ways it has been shared with others.

*Eucharistic Prayer:* Pray with Jesus. Let Jesus standing before the Father raise the deceased person to the Father just as he did at his own death, when he prayed for us all to be forgiven. Lovingly pray with Jesus for the deceased person at the prayer for the departed.

*Communion:* Pray for *healing*. As you go forward to receive Communion, let the deceased go with you. You might imagine him or her standing by your side, or if the deceased is a child you might carry it in your arms. As you receive Communion, ask Jesus to fill you with his healing love in those parts of your being which will still miss the deceased person or still feel wounded by that person. (If possible, after Communion invite those present to lay hands on you and pray for your healing. Communion releases healing power by placing Jesus more deeply within both yourself and those praying for you.) Then let Jesus' precious blood heal all the hurts that may block in you the fullness of Jesus' life. If you are praying for someone in your family line, ask Jesus to let his blood wash away everything negative you have inherited and strengthen all your positive inheritance. Breathe in "Jesus" and breathe out anything negative (fear, anger, negative thoughts, patterns of sin, etc.) until you have no more darkness to breathe out and you are also exhaling the life of Jesus. When you are ready to give life as Jesus, then see his precious blood flow from you to the deceased person, healing all his or her hurts, sinful patterns and occult bondage.* Ask that Jesus' blood flow back through the person's family line to all those living or dead who need Jesus' life. Ask Jesus to show you the prayer in his heart for the deceased, and join Jesus in praying it. If you don't sense Jesus'

---

*Often when occult curses, pacts and seals are enacted, they are repeated three times in mockery of the Trinity. Such involvement by us or our ancestors can be broken by receiving the Eucharist and sincerely praying three times, "In the name of Jesus Christ and through the power of His Precious Blood, I break all curses, pacts, seals or any other occult bondage, especially (specify any known occult bondage), and totally give myself to my Lord Jesus Christ."

prayer for the person, just say "Jesus" silently, exhaling his life into the person and bonding that person by Jesus' blood into Jesus' eternal covenant.

*Blessing:* Gratefully receive all the blessings from Jesus and the deceased as they pray for you. Breathe in their life and with each breath draw closer to Jesus and the deceased.

Although occasionally the results of such a Eucharist have been very dramatic, at other times the Eucharist provides the next step in a gradual healing process. Sometimes, especially in the case of children, you will sense that one Eucharist is enough (this sense may come simply as a feeling of release, completeness or peace when you think of the deceased). At other times you may sense that a deceased person still needs more life or that your own forgiveness of that person needs to deepen. If so, you can continue to pray at the next Eucharist you attend, as did St. Malachy:

### St. Bernard's Account of St. Malachy

The sister of this saint (Malachy) was so worldly-minded that her brother determined not to see her anymore as long as she lived. But although he did not see her in the flesh, he was to see her again in the spirit. After her death, one night he heard a voice telling him that his sister was at the door, complaining that she had had nothing to eat for thirty days. The Saint, when he awoke, forthwith understood what food it was of which she was in need, for it was exactly thirty days since he had offered the sacrifice of the Living Bread for her. He now again began to give her this benefit, which he had withheld from her. Soon he saw her coming up to the church. But she could not yet enter, as she was still wearing a black garment. He continued to offer the holy sacrifice for her every day, and soon saw her a second time, dressed in a lighter garment. Finally, he saw her a third time, clad entirely in white, and surrounded by blessed spirits.[1]

St. Malachy discovered how the Eucharist heals the deceased. Today, many are discovering how the Eucharist for the deceased also heals the living as they come into a deeper relationship with Jesus and the deceased. For example, Dr. Kenneth McAll has more than one thousand cases of emotional or physical healing occurring with his clients primarily through a Eucharist offered for the deceased.[2] Dr. McAll's work has inspired psychotherapy centers such as the Institute for Christian Healing in Philadelphia to frequently encourage their clients to celebrate a Eucharist for deceased loved ones. But if we tried to pray for all the deceased, from the Lazarus we miss the most to the Hitler we most need to forgive, we would be overwhelmed. The following five questions may help to identify who are the most important people to begin bringing to prayer.

1. Whom do I miss the most?
2. Whom have I hurt? Whom do I wish I had done more for?
3. Who hurt me or others? Who had the destructive patterns which have influenced me (e.g., perfectionism, fears, quick temper, etc.)?
4. Who died without a sense of being loved (mentally ill, suicides, victims of violence, babies that were miscarried, aborted or stillborn)?
5. Were any involved in the occult?
6. Who has given me the most gifts and life, my positive heritage?

## Chapter 5

# What About Hell?
# Praying for Great Sinners

Twice during the past year I (Dennis) have visited patients in the hospital who, knowing their time was limited, would ask me, "What would you do if you knew you had only a year left to live?" My answer was immediate both times. "I would write a chapter called 'What About Hell?' and I would spend time visiting people and thanking them for the ways they have loved me."

Perhaps the best way to tell you why this chapter is so important to me is to tell you first about Hilda and then about myself. Hilda asked me for prayer because she was concerned about her suicidal son Robert. Much to my surprise, her question was not, "How can I help him now?" (Later I discovered that Hilda had received counseling for the past several years and was making much progress in relating in healthy ways to Robert, even though her son seldom responded.) Rather, the fright on Hilda's face, the sleepless nights and the weight loss came from her question, "What will happen to Robert if he does take his own life?" So I asked her what she thought would happen. Hilda said, "Since his life is only God's to take, and since he would have no time to repent of such a great sin as suicide, God would condemn him to hell. There would be nothing I could ever do about it, no way I could ever help Robert again." While Hilda was correct in saying that hell is a possibility, she was wrong in putting her son there.

What Hilda believed about Robert going to hell if he committed suicide is what many Christians believed until recently. Until 1800, if a person committed suicide, often his property was confiscated, his body was dragged through the streets and finally his body was burned. [1] Even up to twenty years ago, the body of a suicide was denied Christian burial on consecrated ground because many Christians thought, as Hilda did, that suicides went directly to hell.

We treat suicides differently today because of a change in our understanding of the suicidal person and also in our understanding of God. As doctors like Dr. Stanley Yolles, Director of the National Institute of Mental Health, discover that no healthy person but only a person full of hurts can be driven to suicide,[2] the Church too is discovering that suicide is seldom a deliberate act (mortal sin) of cutting oneself off from God. Usually those who commit suicide are like those in a burning building who feel they have no choice but to jump as the flames come nearer to the windowsill where they stand. They jump, not because they want to cut themselves off from God, but because they see no other way to avoid all the flames about to consume them. We can never know all the pressures that were in another person's life and so we have no right to condemn (Mt 7:1–5).

But the main reason we have no right to condemn a suicidal person or anyone else we consider a "great sinner" is that the Father never condemns. For many centuries, the Western Church emphasized a God who was a condemning judge. In recent years, however, we have come to see God as a merciful healer and we recall the Church's ancient teaching about the mystery of grace. The idea that suicides automatically go to hell is based on a rigid logic that assumes that forgiveness occurs only after repentance. But the mystery of grace is that we are able to repent and change our life only because God has first loved and forgiven us (1 Jn 4:19). It is this mystery of grace that has shaped the Church's teaching about heaven and hell. The Church teaches that heaven exists and that we know at least some of the people who are there: the saints. But while the Church also teaches that an eternal hell exists,[3] "neither Jesus, nor the Church after him, ever stated that persons go there or are actually there now."[3a] In other words, the Church says, "Do not judge who is condemned, but pray for all to receive the Father's love."

Rather than tell Hilda these truths, I wanted her to experience them. So I asked her to close her eyes and imagine that her son had just committed suicide. Then I asked her what she saw. Hilda said she could see Robert approaching the judgment gates where God and St. Peter were waiting to condemn him to hell. Then I asked Hilda to squeeze my hand when she could feel what her son felt. When she squeezed my hand I asked her what her son felt like. "Robert feels so worn out. He has gone through so much pain and hurt." Then I asked her, "What do you want to do as you see your son coming?" Hilda said, "I want to run down and hug him and hold him close to me forever." With that she extended her arms (as if throwing them around Robert's shoulders) and began to cry. Later I asked Hilda, "Do you think God the Father loves Robert as much as you do?" When she nodded I asked, "Then what do you think the Father would do when he saw Robert coming toward him?" Hilda smiled and said, "The Father would do the same thing I did." Then she closed her eyes again and watched as the Father ran down the road to meet Robert. She saw the Father throw his arms around Robert's shoulders and hold Robert close to him. What Hilda saw was no different than the story of the prodigal son, where the Father ran down the road and embraced his worn-out, hurt son. What Hilda's story and the story of the prodigal son tell us is that, contrary to what Hilda and many of us were taught, God the Father is not a condemning judge. Rather, the Father is a merciful healer because he is a lover, and he would respond at least as lovingly as Hilda or the person who loves us most.

### The Prodigal Son Is Jesus' Story About Afterlife

That Hilda wanted to treat her deceased son in the same way the Father treated the prodigal is not a surprise, because the story of the prodigal is the Gospel of Luke's answer to the same question Hilda asked me. The story of the prodigal is not only about how Jesus relates in everyday life to sinners but also about afterlife's messianic banquet thrown by the Father for a son "who was dead and has come back to life" (Lk 15:24, 32).[4]

Luke's Gospel has five consecutive chapters dealing with afterlife, one of which is Chapter 15. In Chapter 15, not only does Luke include the parable of the prodigal son but also two other parables (the lost sheep and the lost coin) dealing with afterlife and especially afterlife's banquet celebrations for repentant sinners. A hint that the three parables' banquet celebrations are afterlife banquets is given by the word *prosdechomai* (welcome). This word is consistently associated in the New Testament with afterlife themes such as the coming of the kingdom or parousia.[5] Luke uses this afterlife word to introduce the three parables and to describe the joy Jesus has in welcoming sinners to the banquet (Lk 15:2). In the first parable, of the lost sheep, the biblical scholar Jeremias sees banquet joy (Lk 15:7) occurring in heaven when a sinner repents in "the last days, the final judgment."[6] The banquet joy in the second parable of the lost coin also takes place before the "angels of God" in heaven whenever a sinner repents (Lk 15:10).

But instead of only repeating the theme of the first two parables concerning the joy in heaven over a repentant sinner, the story of the prodigal son actually takes us to afterlife's messianic banquet so that we can experience how the Father and those in heaven rejoice over one repentant sinner. As in the previous two stories, the prodigal son story also tells us about a loss (not a sheep or a coin, but a lost son), the search, and the joy at finding, and then allows us to experience the rejoicing that goes on at the heavenly banquet over a repentant sinner. What banquet joy when what was lost is found (Lk 15:6, 9, 24, 32)!

But what might surprise us is that the story of the prodigal son is not only about how God loves repentant sinners, but also about how he loves unrepentant sinners. As we will explain, the Father ran down the road and threw his arms around the prodigal son even though, at that point in the story, the prodigal had no intention of repenting. And the father will invite the elder brother to afterlife's banquet, even though the elder brother has not repented. The prodigal son is thus afterlife's story of how the Father loves both the repentant and the unrepentant sinner.

### God Loves the Unrepentant Sinner

That God could love a seemingly unrepentant sinner like Robert was startling not only to Hilda but also to those in Jesus' time. Like those in Jesus' time, Hilda had grown up in a culture based largely on the system of rewards and punishments. In that system, "A's" on report cards are rewards for right answers that bring further rewards from parents, while "F's" are punishments for wrong answers. A hard day's work is rewarded with a paycheck—except in the case of a thief, where it is punished with a jail sentence. But with God, there is no keeping score (Mt 20:1–16). God loves whether a person deserves an "A" and a paycheck or an "F" and a jail sentence. The Father's love is given to all, just as the sun shines and the rain falls on both the just and the unjust. Like many of us, the Pharisees judged Jesus' system unfair. So they asked him such questions as, "How can you welcome tax collectors or other unrepentant sinners and even eat with them?" (Lk 15:1–3). The prodigal son story, where God eats with sinners and not just with the righteous, pharisaical elder brother is Jesus' explanation to the Pharisees about how he welcomes even unrepentant sinners now or in afterlife.

The Pharisees and everyone in the prodigal's village would want the prodigal punished by death because he committed what to the Jews was the worst possible crime, to treat the father of a family as if he were dead. It was inconceivable for any Jew to ask for his father's inheritance while his father was still healthy (let alone spend that inheritance in a Gentile, pagan land). "In all of Middle Eastern literature (aside from the prodigal story) from ancient times to the present, there is no case of any son, older or younger, asking for his inheritance from a father who is still in good health."[7] Thus the prodigal son story is Jesus' story about the greatest possible sinner.

The prodigal son story is radical in proclaiming that God loves not just the greatest possible sinner, but even the unrepentant greatest sinner. The prodigal can be considered unrepentant for two reasons. In the first place, for the rabbis "repentance was primarily a work of man which assured him of God's favor."[8] Before a person was considered to have repented, actions of reparation and atonement were required. Thus, "a shepherd could not fully repent; he did not know how many fields he had trespassed, therefore he could not make adequate reparations." For the Jews listening to Jesus tell the story of the prodigal, therefore, the prodigal would have to make reparations for the lost money *before* he would be considered in a state of repentance.

Secondly, this story is sometimes read as if the prodigal had a change of heart while in the "far country," and planned to ask his father to make him a "hired servant" as a gesture of contrition. Scripture scholarship, however, indicates that the prodigal's motive at this point is more likely self-interest. Although the words of his prepared speech sound like repentance, he composes them after observing that he would get a lot more to eat if he were back in his father's house. He regrets that he has lost all the money he got from his father, but it is unlikely that he has yet repented of breaking his father's heart. The prodigal's lack of repentance for the deeper offense is indicated by his plan to ask his father to make him a "hired servant." In Middle Eastern villages in Jesus' time, the "hired servant" was not considered socially inferior to his employer. The prodigal "will be a free man with his own income living independently in the local village. His social status will not be inferior to that of his father and his brother. He can maintain his pride and his independence." Although the prodigal might intend to use his wages as a "hired servant" to repay his father, in the far country he does not repent of the deeper offense, which is a broken relationship rather than lost money. "He will save himself. He wants no grace."[9] After this unrepentant son has been lovingly welcomed home by his father, he gives only part of his prepared speech, omitting the request that he be made "as one of your hired servants." Why does the prodigal change his speech and end it with "I am no longer worthy to be called your son"? Scholars have often assumed that the prodigal was cut off in mid-speech by the father. But Kenneth Bailey suggests rather that the prodigal chose not to finish his speech because:

> He is shattered by his father's demonstration of love in humiliation. In his state of apprehension and fear he would naturally experience this unexpected deliverance as an utterly overwhelming event. Now he knows that he cannot offer any solution to their ongoing relationship. He sees that the point is not the lost money, but rather the broken relationship which he cannot heal. Now he understands that any new relationship must be a pure gift from his father. He can offer no solution. To assume that he can com-

pensate his father with his labor is an insult. "I am no longer worthy" is now the only appropriate response.[10]

The father offers reconciliation to his son before the prodigal has truly repented and without even asking for a change of heart. Later the father will forgive the elder son before the elder son repents. By arguing with his father in public, the elder son puts a break in the relationship "with his father that is nearly as radical as the break between the father and the younger son at the beginning of the parable."[11] Yet the father will love the unrepentant elder son and promise, even if he doesn't come to the banquet, "Everything I have is yours."

Although the father knows that he can love unrepentant sinners, his main concern is for people who can't. Knowing that his villagers are "score-keepers" who will punish an unrepentant sinner like his son with death, the father keeps daily watch for his son. That is why one day the father can spot the prodigal while his son is still "a long way off." So the father runs to the outskirts of the village. Rather than have the son kiss the father's hand in the customary way, the father "clasped him in his arms and kissed him tenderly." This gesture of "a public kiss by the leading man involved" was only used when a serious quarrel had taken place in the village and only when reconciliation was achieved. Once having placed the family's signet ring on his son's finger and having dressed the son in the family robe, the father knew that under his protective care the son could enter the village unharmed.[12] Thus the father is not concerned about the son repenting, but only in welcoming and protecting the unrepentant sinner.

By having the father throw a party, Jesus is asking the score-keepers among his listeners, "Are you going to keep calculating the score or come to my party?" The elder brother wants to continue keeping score as he complains, "All these years I have slaved for you and never once disobeyed your orders, yet you never offered me so much as a kid for me to celebrate with my friends." At heaven's messianic banquet, from which comes the music and dancing which the elder brother hears as he approaches the house, there is no score keeping. Rather, Jesus wants to extend to the score-keeping Pharisees, to whom he addresses this story, the same invitation that the father extended to the score-keeping elder brother, "Come and eat and welcome the great sinner with me." This acceptance of the unrepentant sinner is echoed many other times in the New Testament and it will continue to scandalize the Pharisees:

> My command to you is: love your enemies, pray for your persecutors. This will prove that you are sons of your heavenly Father, for his sun rises on the bad and the good, he rains on the just and the unjust. If you love those who love you, what merit is there in that? Do not tax collectors do as much? (Mt 5:44–46).

> It is rare that anyone should lay down his life for a just man, though it is barely possible that for a good man someone may have the courage to die. It is precisely in this that God proves his love for us: that while we were still sinners, Christ died for us (Rom 5:7–8).

As you read these Scripture passages or the story of the prodigal, you may wonder how the same God who does such loving things for great sinners can also speak of vindictively punishing great sinners with the everlasting fires of hell (Mt 8:12; 13:42). Perhaps the single greatest need of religious people today, especially in praying for the deceased, is to experience God as a lover who speaks to us and to the deceased in lover's language. Lovers speak in images. When Jesus used

such images as "fire," "everlasting," and "hell," he was speak-
ing as a lover. When we understand Jesus' images, then seem-
ingly vindictive Scripture passages such as those speaking
about the everlasting fire of hell become proclamations of
God's radical care, the merciful care of the prodigal's Father.
Because of the urgent need to interpret all Scripture as "good
news" spoken by a lover, we have written the chapter "What
About Hell? How Can a Loving God Send Anyone There? (A
Scriptural View)" and included it at the end of this book (see
Appendix A).

### Praying for a Deceased Great Sinner

What surprised Hilda most about her prayer for Robert
was that when God the Father threw his arms around Robert,
he loved and forgave Robert in many of the same ways she had.
Hilda, who with the Father welcomed her son, is a model for
how to pray for a great sinner.

Prayer for the deceased is the process of entering into the
presence of the welcoming Father and our deceased loved one
so that like Hilda we can give and receive love and forgiveness.
In such prayer, we become like elder brothers. Standing outside afterlife's messianic banquet, we are given the choice of
judging the prodigal or of welcoming with the Father that
prodigal "who was dead and has come back to life." Such
prayer for the deceased has implications for ourselves as elder
brothers and for the deceased as prodigals.

If as "living" elder brothers we choose not to love and forgive the "deceased" prodigal, we will also be the judging elder
brother standing outside the banquet and putting distance between ourselves and the Father. And the same holds true for
the deceased. If the "deceased" prodigal remains closed to the
elder brother, the prodigal will not be able to be totally at home

with the Father who keeps inviting the elder brother to the eternal banquet.

But when the "deceased" prodigal and the "living" elder brother will love and forgive each other, joy will break out. Just as the joy of the Father and the prodigal will increase each time the elder brother joins them at the banquet table, so will the Father and our deceased loved one's joy increase when in prayer we become present to them in order to give and receive love and forgiveness.

## Great Sinners and the Living

It wasn't Robert's mother or the story of the prodigal that taught me (Dennis) most about how God treats great sinners. Rather the experience of my own general confession was the incident which most changed my life. You may recall that besides writing this chapter, the second thing I would do if I had a year to live would be to visit people and thank them for ways they have loved me. Rightly or wrongly, I feel as though I have given and received more love than any person I know. How radically different I feel now than before my general confession when I didn't like anyone and felt that no one loved me. Before the general confession, I hated myself because I thought that God condemned me. I remember one time, while on vacation, stopping at a gas station and looking at a calendar and at the pornographic picture attached to it. As we were taught that almost all sins regarding sex were very serious, or the kind that merited the eternal fire of hell, during the rest of the trip I lived in fear of dying before I could get to confession. But no matter how many times I went to confession, I never seemed to change. Because I felt constantly condemned, I condemned and hated myself and hated everyone else.

All that changed when I made a general confession of all the sins of my life. I had eight pages, single-spaced, of all the things I hated about myself. After I finished my list, the priest, now probably totally exhausted, came over and hugged me. It was the first time a priest had hugged me. I remember going back to my room and crying. Since I judged so many of the sins to be serious, I had expected the usual sermon about how I had disappointed God and needed to make up my mind to try harder or I would ultimately suffer the painful consequences of hell. But in that hug, I met a God who loved the worst part of myself. Such a lover had not paused first to calculate my score or to see what judgment I might deserve for those eight pages. Ever since that day and those tears, I knew that God never condemned me and that I never needed again to condemn myself or another. Ever since that day I have loved myself and loved, almost immediately, anyone I have met.

I had confessed the same sins many times before and yet was without power to change. No change came because each time before I had met a mercenary God, one who kept score and judged with vengeance. After the general confession it was easy to change and become a loving person without hardly trying. I could love because in that hug I could experience God first loving me (1 Jn 4:19). I wanted to write this chapter before I died because encountering a judging God who kept score and judged with vengeance had brought me twenty years of death, while encountering a God who loved me has now brought me twenty years of life.

## Healing Nations

Welcoming a great sinner as the Father does by not judging with vengeance but rather by loving unconditionally brings healing. Hilda saw how it could bring healing to a deceased son; my confessor saw how it brought me healing. But in Korea I saw how the welcoming of great sinners could even heal a nation. This past summer I experienced how the willingness of the Korean people to welcome a great sinner created a joyous atmosphere, much like the joy at the banquet given for the prodigal's return. I experienced this while watching a TV program which for months was viewed by seventy-five percent of the South Korean audience for up to eighteen hours each day. This program held such universal interest that all other programs were cancelled. Why?

South Korea has at least 100,000 people who were separated from their families during the Korean war when everyone fled in panic to the safety of Pusan Harbor. Day after day these separated people would appear on TV for fifteen seconds carrying a sign stating their name and details about their family and the events that had separated them. If a viewer recognized one of the people on TV, he would call the TV network or go down to the local TV station for a joyful reunion. I and the Koreans never tired of watching these reunions. Five thousand families found each other. As they wept in each other's arms all Korea wept with them. We all watched in awe as the sick forgave the healthy for leaving them behind, children forgave their parents for never returning as promised, and brothers forgave ashamed brothers for cooperating with the North Koreans. For these homecoming lovers, the greater the sinner, it seemed the greater the welcome. Suddenly they were family again, and they could forgive anything. As they forgave each other their great sins, the wounds of war were being healed and a compassionate nation was being reborn. When we welcome as God welcomes, entire nations can be reborn.

### Prayer for Healing the Great Sinner

Jesus, at your eternal banquet you loved the prodigal and elder brother even before they repented.

Show me the deceased loved one that I consider a great sinner.

Let me join you in seeing what hurt he carries in his heart as he comes to you.

Show me what you do to that great sinner as a sign of your love and forgiveness so that I can do the same.

Finally, let me receive your healing mercy into the time I sinned most.

## Chapter 6

# Praying for the Family Tree

Sometimes when I'm in the grocery store, I see a mother dragging her child with one hand and beating it with the other hand, while scolding in a loud voice. I usually think to myself, "I hope your child doesn't grow up to be like you!" One time when I witnessed a scene like this, the grandmother appeared and began scolding the mother in the same harsh voice with which the mother had been scolding the child. So often we find ourselves repeating the same behavior as our parents and grandparents. On the Sioux Indian reservation, often we found that a girl who lived with her alcoholic father and grandfather would marry an alcoholic just like them. Similarly, the Connecticut Department of Corrections found that eighty-one percent of violent sexual offenders had been sexually abused as children, often within the family.[1] How do we stop repeating the same negative behaviors that have been in our families for generations?

I (Sheila) was able to stop repeating a negative behavior pattern in my family only when I extended forgiveness to my father's ancestors and prayed for their healing. My father has a gift of receptivity. He is open to everything around him and able to take in a lot of love. He has passed that gift of receptivity on to me, and I too am open to everything around me and able to take in love from people, nature, music, etc. But the negative side of my father's gift is that he sometimes takes in things he should refuse, such as abuse from those he should have confronted instead. My father's chronic ulcerative colitis seems to be a sign of holding in unexpressed anger. Not only have I inherited my father's gift of receptivity, but I have also inherited his weakness of taking in what should be confronted. Until recently, when someone treated me abusively, I became fright-

75

ened and guilty, assuming that it was my fault. When I looked at this weakness in myself and in my father, I saw that we stand at the end of a long line of people who had this same weakness. Our family is Jewish and for generations many of my people took things in rather than confront because confrontation probably meant death. I found healing and a new ability to confront what should be confronted when I did two things. First, I forgave not only myself and my father but also all the generations of Jews who came before us. Second, I asked Jesus to give me his gift of righteous anger and confrontation, and to extend it backward to all my ancestors.

Several weeks later I found myself able to confront situations where before I would have blamed myself. For instance, I was finally able to write a letter to a committee, objecting to an action they were considering. It was an unusually direct letter for me, but I felt new courage to speak the truth as I saw it. One of the committee members, whose ancestry is German, objected to my having written the letter and said that I should have cooperated with the committee instead. I felt sudden, overwhelming anger at this man, more intense than all my feelings about the committee's plans. When I began to pray about my anger, I was amazed to hear myself say, "Your people told my people to cooperate—and my people got it!" Although I have never experienced anti-semitism personally and none of my immediate family were killed in concentration camps, I was somehow carrying a hurt inflicted upon my ancestors. I knew that before I could be at peace with the German committee member, I had to forgive his German ancestors on behalf of my Jewish ancestors. So I prayed for his family line in the same way I prayed for my own family several weeks earlier. I forgave the Germans and asked for healing of all hurts which had led them to kill Jews. The next time I met with this man we discussed the same issues. Even though he still criticized my letter in the same way, I no longer felt overwhelming anger at him. Like my previous fear of confrontation, my excessive anger at the German man was a problem that could be traced back to deceased people I had never known.

## Psychological Basis for Ancestral Prayer

Although it is dangerous to trace all psychological problems back to the deceased, the new field of family psychotherapy confirms that it is equally dangerous to ignore the effect of past generations upon present emotional conflicts. Family therapists from many psychotherapeutic traditions look not just at the isolated patient but also at how the patient's illness expresses the invisible conflicts and loyalties among family members, some of whom are even deceased. Family therapists trace the interaction patterns that are handed down from grandfather to father to son. The son is likely to raise his own children in his father's shadow by either making the same mistakes or by overreacting and making the opposite mistakes. Psychologist W. Hugh Missildine even states that in every marriage there are really six people: the married couple and each of their parents.[2] So, for example, when a wife asks her husband to empty his ashtray and he explodes with, "You have ordered me around all my life—all my married life," he may be projecting on his wife the anger he feels toward his dominating mother.

Other therapists such as Bowen find that not only marital conflicts but also serious illnesses such as schizophrenia often have their roots in three or more generations of family dynamics which have frustrated individuation in a child commanded to mature but kept immature by immature parents.[3] Bowen finds that the less a person is individuated (i.e., has developed his unique, true self), the more he can be influenced by others until he finally develops an illness which expresses the problems of those around him. He is the "identified patient," when really it is the whole family that is ill.

Because of this "multigenerational structure" in much emotional illness, more and more therapists insist on working with a family unit of at least three generations rather than treating an isolated individual.

> Our growing conviction of the importance of loyalty and justice networks in families has coincided with our belief that the minimal context of therapy should be the three-generational family unit. Working exclusively with the nuclear family could ultimately amount to implicit, technical scapegoating of the parents as originators of a detrimental, unjust treatment of their children. We have learned that all noxious relationship patterns have a multigenerational structuring.[4]

Unfortunately, family therapists have found that the person who is least aware of how he is influenced by past generations is often the person most manipulated by them.

> The less he is aware of the invisible obligations accumulated in the past, for instance, by his parents, the more he will be at the mercy of these invisible forces. In families the system unit of accounting tends to include generations. According to the Scriptures seven generations may balance out one major sin of an ancestor.
>
> The family therapist must learn how to reconstruct a minimally three-generational balancing of accounts of justice. Children can be blamed for their solidarity with their parents by the grandparents who consider the parents disloyal to themselves and

their family (e.g., in matters of religion or other tradition). The child, then, unconsciously may fit into a strategy for the exoneration of the parents or perpetuate the guilt encumbrance through the following generation. Further examples could be given of daughters who were raised by "respectable" relatives because of their mother's "life of shame" and who decide to seek out and join their mothers; of sons who suffer while hiding the secret of their mother's suspected murder by father's girlfriend. Ultimately, the greatest relief these children can find lies in the vindication in their own eyes of their parents through understanding the unfairness of the circumstances which led their parents to their condemnable actions.[5]

The reason the "condemnable actions" of our ancestors may continue to affect us "unto the seventh generation" is not because God punishes innocent descendants. Rather, it is because we tend to repeat whatever we do not forgive. Whether our parents were overly possessive or neglectful, they and their ancestors who taught them need to be understood, forgiven and vindicated or else our reaction to their mistakes will need the forgiveness of our children—or even seven generations of children.

## The Interface Between Family Therapy and Prayer

The process of family therapy involves steps of building rapport between the family members and the therapist, recalling family history, taking responsibility for perpetuating destructive family patterns, and owning family strengths while developing constructive new family patterns. These steps of family therapy can be used jointly with the three steps of prayer introduced in Chapter 4:

1. Share your heart (developing rapport) with Jesus by recalling memories of deceased family members and thus allowing Jesus to grieve with you. As you recall memories, you may find a need to forgive Jesus (e.g., for the family he put you in, for allowing a particular family member to die, etc.).

2. Unbind deceased family members by giving and receiving forgiveness for destructive family patterns.

3. Give thanks for the gifts, constructive patterns and positive heritage that have come or can come to you and future generations from the deceased.

Last Father's Day, Dennis and I (Matt) used these three steps to pray for our father's side of the family. Perhaps as important as the prayer itself was our preparation for that prayer. We prepared by gathering photos and mementos that recalled to our hearts stories about various family members. For instance, my grandmother's gentle, sun-tanned photo recalls how she and her children worked in the garden and then gave most of the food away to neighbors. Her generous reputation attracted company every Sunday, and the company would get the best portions at dinner. In stark contrast to my grandmother, my grandfather's photo, which portrays him with a gothic scowl and a rifle in his hands, reveals a strict disciplinarian. When I look at my grandfather's face, I believe my Dad's story about how my grandfather raised seventeen children without ever raising his voice. When he wanted to discipline one of his children, all he had to do was give his stern "be careful" look and the child would immediately obey him. I am

sure those words were handed down from his voiceless ancestors who, living on the Franco-German border with constant
invasions, tried with stern faces to say "be careful" to their
French and German occupant invaders. Every time our ancestors' goods were taken as the spoils of war, their faces became
sterner and their desire for law and order more intense. As we
lined up other photos of those in my father's family tree, both

the photos and the stories they provoked added to our understanding of our grandparents.

We began to make a list of the family members for whom
we especially wanted to pray as our hearts opened more and
more to those in our father's family tree. Preparing in this way
helped us create an atmosphere of love. This atmosphere of
love provided a clear channel of connection between our hearts
and the hearts of the deceased in our family tree.

So, when we were finally ready to pray, we began by inviting Jesus to connect our hearts with the hearts of those in
the family tree. Then we recalled with Jesus the special ways
he cared for each of them, beginning with our great-grandfather who was born six months after his father's death. If his
father had died three months earlier, none of us would be here.
As we gave thanks for each person, I was aware of how different this prayer was from the one I had prayed for my father's
family tree several years ago. At that time, my cousin Fr. Joe
had just died. I loved Fr. Joe and he had been a model of priest-
hood for me. During my prayer several years ago, I spent
much of it not only grieving with Jesus for the ways I missed
Fr. Joe but also healing my relationship with Jesus. Why did
Jesus say, "I will be with you always" (Mt 28:20) and then not
protect Fr. Joe from evil? I forgave Jesus and his father for taking such a young, generous priest friend as Fr. Joe from me,
while leaving many cranky priests to seemingly live forever.
Whether it is by giving thanks for my great-grandfather's birth
or by forgiving Jesus and his Father for Fr. Joe's death, the first
step is one of building rapport with Jesus so that with him I
can embrace my entire family tree.

As Jesus began to embrace with me my entire family tree,
I knew that not only I but also my ancestors felt safe. Once
such a safe atmosphere was established, I was ready to begin
step two, the recognition of destructive patterns. In such an
atmosphere I could acknowledge the perfectionism in me that

says "be careful" and that puts on a stern face when my expectations and need for order are not met. For example, if the
phone rings when I am writing, I find my teeth grinding as my
sense of order and creativity are interrupted. "Be careful"
makes me feel that I must read another book before I can write
anything well, and I keep sending revisions to the publisher up
to and past the final moment. I may laugh at the perfectionism
in my father who doesn't want any dandelions on his lawn and
is always cleaning what is already clean, but it is in me too.

So on Father's Day I lifted up to Jesus my perfectionism
that comes from always trying to "be careful," and the stern
face I get when my expectations and need for order are not met.
I asked forgiveness and healing for the ways I have allowed
these patterns to be embodied in me more than Dennis has. I
asked for the gift of gratitude so that I could see and affirm the
positive rather than immediately focus on what is or could go
wrong. I breathed in from Jesus his ability to be open to the
present moment and his willingness to be constantly interrupted by people in need such as Jairus. When I felt filled with
Jesus' power to love, I breathed his love and forgiveness into
my father. When I sensed he was filled with peace, I moved
on to my grandfather, great-grandfather and other Linn ancestors the Lord alone knew—a faceless crowd Jesus wanted to
heal. I was led to breathe with Jesus his healing forgiveness into
the German and French soldiers who had persecuted my
ancestors. These soldiers too were driven by a perfectionism
that made them try to prove their superiority through con-
quest. Then I recalled again the picture of my stern, gun-toting
grandfather. I sensed that he was grateful I understood, and
that he was promising to protect me as he stood with his gun
by Jesus' side.

That brought me to step three, which is giving thanks. I
thanked my grandfather for his protection and for his farmer's
love of the land. I shared with him that during my thirty-day

retreat, the times that I felt closest to my Creator were the times I planted marigold seeds and carefully nurtured them into life. I could feel God's love nurturing me as I lovingly nurtured the spindly seedlings. I gave thanks for the patient care I have for seedlings or for people broken by life's hurts—the care flowing from my perfectionism that wants to heal disorder. I continued for a few minutes to silently breathe in all the gifts and love Jesus was giving me through my grandfather and his family. I thanked Jesus that my grandfather and all those with him in heaven would now intercede and be channels of healing love for all their relatives wounded by perfectionism. I asked that they continue to be channels of healing love to future unborn generations. My grandfather was no longer a stern, gun-toting disciplinarian, but rather a fatherly channel of Jesus' love leading us all closer to each other and to Jesus.

### Relationships Most Needing Prayer

Since we are each related to millions of ancestors, how do we determine which of our many relationships with deceased family members most need prayer? The following questions may help you identify those in your family most needing healing prayer.

1. Whom do you miss the most in your family? (E.g., Matt's relationship with John Thomas described in Chapter 2.)

2. Whom have you hurt? For whom do you wish you had done more?

3. Who hurt you or others? Who had the destructive patterns which have influenced you (e.g., perfectionism, fear of confrontation, quick temper, stinginess, alcoholism, etc.)?

4. Who were the most unloved people in your family? Who died without a sense of being cared for (e.g., suicides, sudden or violent deaths, victims of war, the mentally ill)? Who was unknown or unwanted (e.g., miscarried, aborted or stillborn babies)? (See Chapter 7.)

5. Has anyone in your family been involved in the occult?

6. Which family members have given you the most gifts and life (your positive heritage)?

The rest of this chapter will take each of these relationships and illustrate it with an example of how prayer healed such a relationship. Much of the material will be drawn from the work of psychiatric consultant Dr. Kenneth McAll, who in over twenty years has amassed over one thousand cases of people helped by prayer for their ancestors.[6]

### 1. Whom do you miss most in your family?

Those we love and miss the most can leave us with deep wounds or, when the wound of grief is healed, with deep gifts as did the death of my brother John described in Chapter 2. Recently I developed another gift, the art of CPR (cardio-pulmonary resuscitation). The course was taught using a mannequin, Resusciannie, that responded only if the CPR technique was right. A bereft father invented Resusciannie after his daughter Annie drowned in a swimming pool because neither he nor anyone else knew how to do CPR to revive her. Rather than continually focus on how he didn't revive her, Annie's father healed his grief by building Resusciannie to teach CPR nationwide. The Resusciannie mannequin is even dressed in the red and blue outfit Annie died in as a reminder of how her death is bringing forth new life. This is in stark contrast to the seventy-five percent of parents who lose a child over four years old and are so wounded by unhealed grief that their marriages end in divorce. Those we love most leave the deepest wounds and the deepest gifts.

Sometimes the death of a loved one leaves a very subtle wound. As Joan began seeing a counselor, she became aware of an ever present sadness. Joan also suffered from chronic arthritis. But the sadness was immune to counseling and the arthritis was immune to medical treatment until Joan prayed with a friend about the origin of her problems. They asked Jesus, "Why this sadness, Lord?" Jesus led them back to the memory of Joan's loving grandmother dying when Joan was only three. Joan loved her grandmother who had her personality, the same blue eyes, and a lap eager to hold her. Joan felt for the first time her anger at her grandmother and God for the death of the one she counted upon. Slowly she began to forgive God and her grandmother for the loss she had never grieved. As she let go, she opened her hands and found her painful arthritis healed, and it remains healed to this day.

## 2. *Whom have you hurt? For whom do you wish you had done more?*

In most cases of prolonged grief, there is remorse that "I should have . . ." Dr. Kenneth McAll shares how an eighty-six year old World War I veteran lost his right arm to a shell which killed his four best friends. Daily he suffered excruciating attacks of phantom arm pain eased only by addiction to the pain-killer drug physeptone. He shared how his friends never had a funeral nor had he prayed for them, because while he lost only an arm, "there was nothing to bury" of his friends. With Dr. McAll's suggestion that he could pray for them and commit them to God, his destructive guilt over being the sole survivor vanished and his severe arm pain never returned despite discontinuing physeptone.[7]

### 3. Who hurt you or others?

As in the case of the man with phantom arm pain, in praying for a person we have hurt or failed, we need to forgive ourselves. In praying for a person who hurt or failed us, we need to forgive that person by joining Jesus to hate the sin but to love the sinner. We can forgive another only when we can see ourselves as equally in need of Jesus' mercy, if only in our very struggle to forgive. In the example of Bob (Chapter 4) struggling to forgive Hitler, Bob was not an insane mass murderer like Hitler. But Bob's breakthrough in compassionately forgiving Hitler came when he saw how his own hard-heartedness toward Hitler was at least something like Hitler's hard-heartedness toward millions of Jews. Sometimes we are led to pray for ancestors whose destructive patterns we can see clearly in ourselves. At other times we are led to pray for ancestors who were destructive in ways very unlike ourselves. However unlike them we are, the key to compassion and forgiveness is to see our own need for healing as well, if only in our struggle to love such unloving people. If we do not first seek insight and healing for our own destructiveness, we simply blame others and avoid responsibility to change. But when we see our own need for Jesus' mercy, we are able to compassionately extend it to others.

To discover who in our family has hurt us by handing on destructive patterns, it often helps to construct a family tree. Although Americans can seldom remember beyond four generations, Dr. McAll in his work with British families has run across many patterns tracing back to the eighteenth century and healed through a Eucharist for the deceased. Although ancestral prayer is primarily for healing ordinary inherited patterns such as perfectionism, even deep disturbances can respond to prayer.

> Margaret was seventy-three years old when her "attacks" began suddenly. Violent outbursts of temper, unprovoked aggression towards her younger sister Nellie with whom she lived, bouts of smashing objects without any conscious intent were quite uncharacteristic of her. Their mother who had died four years previously, aged ninety-six, had behaved in a similar way. After each attack, Margaret was full of apologies and genuinely remorseful but unable to offer any explanation.
>
> So we drew up their Family Tree [see below] in as much detail as we could and a strange pattern emerged. For the past six generations the eldest female in the family had shown signs of similarly disturbed behaviour. This trait had begun in about 1750 when a murder had been committed in the family. Then the eldest daughter, Elizabeth, became an alcoholic and destroyed much family property before she drank herself to death at the age of forty. Subsequently, each eldest daughter in the family had had violent temper tantrums at the slightest provocation down to Margaret, my patient, who was born in 1904.
>
> Margaret's niece, Rhonda, the eldest daughter of her youngest sister, was born in 1941 and was thirty-two years old. She had been having psychiatric treatment for several months before Margaret's case was brought to me. Rhonda had only agreed to this treatment after her husband had returned home one eve-

ning to find badly damaged furniture, broken windows and a generally chaotic situation and had threatened to walk out and start divorce proceedings, taking the children with him. She realized that she needed help and agreed to see a psychiatrist. . . .

We decided to offer a Eucharist for Rhonda and for the eldest females of the preceding six generations. With two clergymen, one doctor, two nurses, Nellie [Margaret's younger sister] and myself, we held a service for these family ancestors who apparently had contributed to this chain of violent temper tantrums. Although it was held in private, without the knowledge of my patient Margaret, or her niece Rhonda, neither woman has had any further attacks. Rhonda's behaviour became entirely normal and her husband dropped his threatened divorce suit. Their marriage was able to settle down normally. Margaret once again became a caring elder sister and Nellie's troubles were at an end.

There are two main objectives in constructing a family tree. First, to establish whether any ancestor showed evidence of the same unacceptable behaviour; secondly, to ascertain whose voice, whose unquiet spirit is speaking to and through the person seeking help—the patient.[8]

Notice the steps Dr. McAll takes. After a thorough medical and psychiatric examination, he draws up a family tree. This is very helpful for seeing problems and their patterns as well as for specifying who should receive prayer. (Often it is the most sensitive child or the eldest who is most open to transmitting parental patterns.) At special Eucharists for the deceased (see Chapter 4), this tree is placed upon the altar or held

## The Family Tree of Margaret and Rhonda

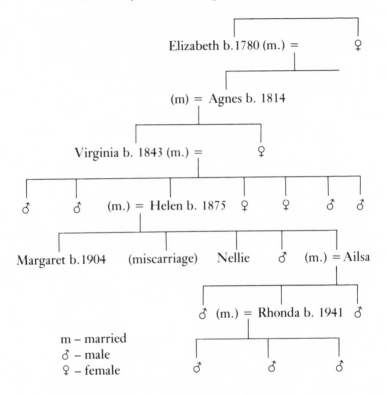

in the client's hands. Usually the more the client can love and forgive the ancestors, the more healing occurs in the client. But note that although neither Margaret nor Rhonda was present or even aware of the Eucharistic service for their ancestors, their attacks ceased with the service. Dr. McAll's many experiences with those absent being immediately healed has led him to suggest that the healing may come not only from psychologically working through the relationship at the service but also from the deceased ancestor being healed and empowered to reach out lovingly toward even those not present at the service.

4. *Who were the most unloved people in your family? Who died without a sense of being cared for (e.g., suicides, sudden or violent deaths, victims of war, the mentally ill)? Who was unknown or unwanted (e.g., miscarried, aborted or stillborn babies)?*

When searching the family tree, Dr. McAll looks for who was most unloved. One of his most mind-boggling cases is that of Edward whom we met while visiting Dr. McAll's patients in England. As Dr. McAll checked through medical records and spoke with Edward and his wife, he discovered that Edward had many symptoms. To begin with, not only did Edward feel a yellow band around his head and smell sulphur but he also heard explosions which made him feel split in two and filled with fire from head to toe. Besides hearing explosions, he heard waves crashing, voices of men shouting, and wind whistling across his face and feet. For these symptoms Edward had received thirty years of psychiatric treatment from other doctors, including ECT, antidepressants, drugs for schizophrenia and sedatives. Though Edward was still experiencing all these symptoms despite years of treatment, the symptom most worrying him was a sweating attack of a few nights before. For several nights, climaxing on November 11, for no apparent reason Edward had developed a high fever and began to sweat so profusely that he changed the bed linen several times. The severity of it as well as the suddenness of the onset concerned him.

After listening to the symptoms and doing an extensive medical check-up, Dr. McAll altered his method of listening. Instead of asking about members of the family tree, Dr. McAll simply said, "It sounds like pirates." Edward suddenly stopped looking at his feet and became very alert, as he asked: "Do you know what my last name is?" Dr. McAll went over to the chart on his desk and read the last name "Hawkins." Edward, as Dr. McAll was to discover, was a direct descendant of eight pirate captains and thirty other seamen who died at sea. Upon further research in the encyclopedia, they discovered that Captain Sir John Hawkins died at sea November 11, 1595 from a tropical fever while trying to rescue his son, Richard. November 11 was the same day that Edward Hawkins experienced the climax of his feverish attack.

After praying for Sir John Hawkins and his pirate ancestors, all the symptoms that Edward had struggled with for twenty years stopped. During the first Eucharists, Jesus gathered mainly the Hawkins captains and seamen. But during the more recent Eucharists, Jesus seems to focus on the frightened victims of the Hawkins expeditions including crews of ships that were sunk and captives that were forced to walk the gangplanks.

Edward's Eucharists touched the deceased and the living. Besides freeing Edward from thirty hellish years of schizophrenic living, there was an immediate change in Edward's wife and parents. His wife, in her late thirties, had tried for years to conceive a child but without any success. Several weeks after the Eucharist freed her husband, she found that she had conceived a child. Edward's mother also called that same week with the exciting news that Edward's father who had suffered a long term depression had said "thank you" and "had begun to laugh at jokes and be content at home."

It is difficult for me to believe that a death not grieved some four hundred years ago can have an impact today on Edward and his family. The story of Margaret helps me see how yesterday's buried grief becomes acted out in today's descendants. Every February Margaret became depressed. By February 14 the depression would become so severe that she would have to be hospitalized. What surprised Margaret and everyone was that during the rest of the year she was full of life working as a full time nurse. In the depth of her depression one February 14, she prayed with a friend for Jesus to reveal the root hurt. They both saw an image of her mother miscarrying a child. Jesus revealed that the miscarriage took place eighteen months before Margaret's birth and that her mother had buried the grief and tried to conceive another child. The result was Margaret, who like any fetus shared her mother's hormones and therefore her mother's buried grief. Margaret and her friend prayed for Jesus to love and heal the miscarried child, and then they prayed for Margaret to be filled with joy from the first moment of conception. Margaret felt an immediate release from the depression and it has never returned. After the prayer, her aunt verified that her mother had miscarried eighteen months before Margaret's birth. The aunt remembered the date because it was Valentine's Day (February 14), the date also of Margaret's annual depression.

If Margaret had not grieved for her mother's miscarried child, would Margaret's descendants have found themselves depressed on February 14? How did the symptoms of pirates get passed on to Edward? I am not sure how such a hurt is passed on and acted upon generations later. There can be many explanations: McAll's belief in an ancestor crying out for prayer, our projections of our evil that are healed by intercession for another who is like us, the transmission of memories by genes or learning to a child, Jung's collective unconscious, the healing of the memory of our unfinished business, etc. Perhaps all of these are true. I tend to believe that in prayer we are touching not only a memory in a living person but also a deceased person who through Jesus receives love and then becomes in turn a loving intercessor. It may also be that we are sensing how the deceased needs healing just as when we are with a living depressed person and find ourselves feeling more depressed. But even if the departed no longer need prayer in the way we are led to pray, they still sense our love through Jesus and are further empowered to love us and others in need of healing. Whatever the explanation, we agree with Fr. William Johnston, an expert on Eastern mysticism, that when the Spirit heals us, the Spirit is healing wounds that go back generations and touch multitudes.

> The hurts and pains that have been lurking in the psyche from early childhood, from the moment of birth, from the time in the womb, from the moment of conception—all of these are floating to the surface and are being healed by the love of the indwelling Spirit in whose presence one quietly sits. Furthermore, while I myself cannot accept a literal interpretation of the Buddhist doctrine of past lives and of liberation from bad *karma*, I think I understand what Buddhists are driving at; and I see there is a valuable insight. For I believe that there takes place a healing of something more than my little ego with its memory of a mere forty, fifty or sixty years. There is more to it than this. There is a healing of the archetypes, of the collective unconscious, of the wounds I have inherited from my ancestors. There is a healing of the cosmic dimension of the psyche; there is a healing of the basic human condition which we call original sin.[9]

The healing of Edward and his pirate ancestors may not be the unusual but the usual. No man is an island but through Jesus is related to everyone in all centuries.

The ties that relate us to everyone in all centuries is the theme of Madeleine L'Engle's remarkable fictional novel, *A*

*Swiftly Tilting Planet.* As the story begins, the world is about to be destroyed by Madog Branzillo, a mad South American dictator. Fifteen year old Charles Wallace is sent on a rescue mission through time to save the world, accompanied by a unicorn, his sister Meg's intercession, and an ancient prayer calling on all the powers of God. Charles is sent to enter four people, from Madoc, a young man in an ancient Welsh village, to Madoc's descendant, Chuck Maddox, a boy who lives in early twentieth century America. Each of the four people faces a crisis that could bring evil upon many others. In each case, Charles recites the prayer at a critical moment, and the impending evil with all its hurtful consequences is averted. Meanwhile, Meg learns that all four of the people Charles enters are ancestors of Madog Branzillo. When Charles returns from his journey through time, he is astonished to learn that Branzillo is now a respected world leader known for his commitment to peace. In this novel about the mysterious web that binds us all together across time and space, healing love offered to ancestors who lived in the distant past has healing consequences that echo across many centuries.[10]

Yet most of us cannot recall any ancestors beyond three generations. Jesus simply asks us to pray for those unknown ancestors who were unable to give and receive love because they felt unloved or were traumatized. Some may have felt unloved because they were betrayed, beaten, raped, entangled in incest, alcoholism, or perhaps even mental illness. Public shame, grinding poverty, war traumas or natural disasters may have traumatized others. Jesus wants to bring his love into any event which left a person feeling helpless, trapped, isolated, fearful or stricken in the ability to return to normal life. As we pray for the healing of the injured and forgive the injuring party, Jesus replaces the negative influence with his healing love flowing down to all generations.

**5. Has anyone in your family been involved in the occult?**

The occult refers to practices which seek power or knowledge from a source contrary to God's teachings (Dt 5:6–10; 18:10–12). For instance, astrology, ouija boards, automatic writing, horoscopes, fortune telling, divination, seances, tarot cards, transcendental meditation, witchcraft, and demonic curses can open up devotees to evil spirits and their dark, occult world. For how to pray for this inherited openness to the occult, see Appendix C.

Perhaps it seems unjust that we and even children are affected by the occult worship of our ancestors.[11] But in the same passage which promises that occult worship will affect even the fourth generation, Yahweh promises mercy to the thousandth generation of those who love him.

> I, the Lord, am your God who brought you out of the land of Egypt, that place of slavery. You shall not have other gods besides me. You shall not carve idols for yourselves in the shape of anything in the sky above or on the earth below or in the waters beneath the earth: you shall not bow down before them or worship them. For I, the Lord, your God, am a jealous God, inflicting punishment for their fathers' wickedness on the children of those who hate me, down to the third and fourth generation; but bestowing mercy down to the thousandth generation on the children of those who love me and keep my commandments (Ex 20:2–6).

In the New Testament, St. Paul also stresses the power of those who love God to bless the others in the family line.

> The unbelieving husband is consecrated by his believing wife; the unbelieving wife is consecrated by

her believing husband. If it were otherwise, your children should be unclean; but as it is, they are holy (1 Cor 7:14).

The good news is that we can bless each other more abundantly than we can curse each other (Heb 7:5–10).

### 6. Which family members have given you the most gifts and life (your positive heritage)?

I (Matt) experienced my positive heritage when I prayed in the church of my forefathers in Glendalough, Ireland. The Irish side of my family has deep faith practiced in daily Mass, attendance at forty hours devotion, and trust in prayer. As I entered St. Kevin's Church in Glendalough, I found the church full of people praying silently during the forty hours veneration of the Blessed Sacrament. I knew that my American-born mother and grandmother and generations in Ireland had done the same. I felt that the church was filled not just with living people but with past generations of saints who had passed on their faith and were interceding for their descendants.

I felt a wave of intercession pour into me filling me with love of Jesus and the Blessed Sacrament. I asked Jesus to open me to all the good in my family line and to cleanse me of any evil. Then I thanked Jesus for all the relatives I could remember who had passed on to me their Irish faith. Slowly I felt filled with a faith that could convert the world. Then it dawned on me that it was from Glendalough that the Irish monks set out to convert Europe and the known world. I was receiving the faith heritage of my ancestors with their special gift of mission to all nations. Since that time our ministry has taken on a new worldwide dimension in over thirty countries. The Irish monks specialized in confession and reconciliation as we do too. I am sure that much of our ministry must be credited to the intercession of my Irish ancestors. As I become more grateful for them and pray for them, I move more deeply into their gifts. Slowly I am also moving into the gift of intercession by praying with them and with their faith for past, present and future Irish generations.

While prayer helps me move into my Irish heritage, so do other activities. An Irish friend plants potatoes each year to deepen his love for his ancestors. I find it easier to bask in my ancestors' Irish love while eating potatoes, enjoying hot tea in winter, discussing politics into the night, and trying to choose, as they did, another rainy day.

We find that we experience the gifts of our positive heritage more deeply as we share them with each other. I (Sheila) have a gift of seeing God's goodness in all things, a gift from my Jewish ancestors who emphasized a God who "saw everything that he had made and indeed it was very good" (Gen 1:31). As we receive this gift from generations of Jews, all three of us become more able to love and affirm creation. Dennis has a gift of celebration from the Irish side of his ancestry, with their love for music and parties. The more we love Dennis' Irish ancestors, the more Matt and I are healed of our tendency to overwork and the more all of us learn to celebrate and enjoy life. Matt has a gift of searching for truth and stating it in precise ways, a gift from the precise and orderly German side of his ancestry. As we honor Matt's care and precision in speaking and writing, we are all receiving life from his German ancestors. Furthermore, as the three of us grow in learning to love each other and draw forth each other's gifts, we believe that ancient hurts between Jews, Irish and Germans are being healed and our ancestors are drawn deeper into Jesus' heart where they too can love each other and draw forth each other's gifts.

Our positive heritage may include not only our ancestors but also those members of the communion of saints who founded and cared for any group to which we belong. Just as Matt and Dennis and I can share the gifts of our ancestry with one another, we can also share other forms of positive heritage. For example, I experience Matt and Dennis sharing with me their Jesuit heritage. Since we became friends and began working together, I've noticed that living Jesuits often feel like brothers to me as soon as I meet them. But more than that, I've also noticed the brotherly presence to me of St. Ignatius and other deceased Jesuits whenever I am in a Jesuit house. This sense of their spiritual presence has grown to the point that I recognize it immediately and because of it I can tell the difference between Jesuit houses and other religious houses. Increasingly I also sense this presence watching over me in other situations and I've learned to consciously open myself to it when I need the charisms of St. Ignatius and other great Jesuits, such as discernment of spirits or praying with Scripture. I find that as I become one in friendship with Matt and Dennis, I am drawn into their Jesuit heritage and personally cared for by Jesuit members of the communion of saints.

## Abuses in Praying for Ancestors

Sometimes when we speak about praying for ancestors, people get fascinated and look upon it as the magical solution for all their problems. Ten years ago when many Christian groups rediscovered the reality of evil spirits, some thought that deliverance ministry would solve all their problems. Today some who become fascinated with ancestors exhaust themselves in the process of ferreting out the pirates or other unknown ancestors needing prayer. Others think it a magical process where all they need to do is write down the names and then find someone to celebrate a Eucharist for each person on their list. Though some healing may happen, usually more healing happens the more we become responsible for giving and receiving love with Jesus and the deceased. Fascination and magical solutions either make us overly responsible or make us shirk responsibility altogether rather than take proper responsibility for giving and receiving love with our deceased loved ones.

Praying for ancestors easily becomes unbalanced through over-responsibility. One lady lamented, "It was enough to deal with my own problems, and now I have to deal with all the problems of all my ancestors." Jesus asks us to let him be the Savior and to pray for the one or two people he places in our heart. The key is not knowing everything about the family tree but rather, with Jesus, loving deeply those we know. Knowing those we are praying for helps us forgive and love them more deeply, but we can also ask Jesus to love those we don't even know.

Just as we are not responsible to deal with all our ancestors, we are not responsible for all their problems. Sometimes a person committing suicide leaves a note stating why others made him take his life. This is a guilt trap. We can not force another to commit suicide any more than we can keep him from taking his life if he chooses to try suicide. We can only offer a person opportunities to be healed, but what he does with the opportunities is up to him. If people were so malleable and easily determined by others, they would get well overnight when offered help. If we have made mistakes, then we are to hate the sin, repent, and love ourselves as sinner rather than perpetually castigate ourselves for not being the Savior Jesus alone can be.

The second abuse is to shirk our proper responsibility. A depressed man once told me, "I am depressed because I grew up as an orphan never knowing a parent's love. I can't do anything to change that." But I also know a loving couple who have been foster parents for fifteen hundred children in the last fifteen years. When I asked why they did this, they answered, "We both grew up as orphans disliking our parents who abandoned us. When we could finally forgive them, we were freed to love again and determined that we would give to other children the love we didn't receive." Hurts affect us but do not determine us. We all have free will. We are responsible for how we continue to let the resentment grow and cripple us further rather than with Jesus' power give and receive forgiving love so that the hurt becomes gift.

As we learn to lovingly forgive the deceased and those who hurt them we receive the gift of loving all of life as did Wild Bill.

Wild Bill was one of the inmates of the concentration camp, but obviously he hadn't been there long: his posture was erect, eyes bright, energy indefatigable. Since he was fluent in English, French, German, and Russian, as well as Polish, he became an unofficial camp translator. Though he worked fifteen and sixteen hours a day, he showed no signs of weariness. While the rest of us were dropping with fatigue, he seemed to gather more strength.

I was astonished to learn, when Wild Bill's own papers came before us one day, that he had been in Wuppertel since 1939! For six years he had lived on the same starvation diet, slept in the same airless and disease-ridden barracks as everyone else, but without the least physical or mental deterioration. Wild Bill was our greatest asset, reasoning with the different groups, counseling forgiveness.

"It's not easy for some of them to forgive," I commented to him one day, "So many of them have lost members of their families."

"We lived in the Jewish section of Warsaw," he began slowly, the first words I had ever heard him speak about himself, "my wife, our two daughters, and our three little boys. When the Germans reached our street they lined everyone against a wall and opened up with machine guns. I begged to be allowed to die with my family, but because I spoke German they put me in a work group."

"I had to decide right then," he continued, "whether to let myself hate the soldiers who had done this. It was an easy decision, really. I was a lawyer. In my practice I had seen too often what hate could do to people's minds and bodies. Hate had just killed the six people who mattered most to me in the world. I decided then that I would spend the rest of my life— whether it was a few days or many years—loving each person I came in contact with."[12]

To love each person, the living and the dead, leads to life here and hereafter.

### Prayer for Healing My Family Tree

Jesus, you inherited the special Jewish gifts of faith, perseverance, and strong family ties.

Show me the gift I have inherited that you most appreciate (e.g., deep Irish faith, German industriousness).

Let me join you in thanking each of the family members who gave me those gifts.

Jesus, only your mother was born without sin, and even from her womb she gave you perfect love.

Show me a hurt from my family tree that continues to cripple me (e.g., Irish melancholy, German perfectionism).

Let me join you as you breathe healing into me and the family members who passed on that hurt to me.

Chapter 7

# Healing Relationships with Miscarried, Aborted and Stillborn Babies*

---

*A reprint of this chapter is available in booklet form entitled AT PEACE WITH THE UNBORN. A condensation in leaflet form is also available, entitled "Healing Relationships with Miscarried, Aborted and Stillborn Babies." See pages 243 and 245.

# Prayer for a Miscarried Child

Praise God for His gentle Love,
 beyond our understanding;
For His Love that conceived you, a perfect child,
 beautiful, unique, and whole,
For His Love that longed to share with you
 the wonders of creation,
For His Love that waited—
 for just the right time,
  for just the right parents,
   for you.

But something happened
 before you were born.
The sin in this world
 attacked your small life—
Weakening, dimming
 your bright little spark.

God had to decide
 on the more loving course:
To heal you in this life,
 and to let you be born;
Or to call you to Himself—
 to hold you in His arms,
 and to heal you with a kiss.

It's hard for us to understand
 why God healed you the way He did.
Often we wish that you were here;
 that you didn't die so young.
So please ask Jesus to help us
 to see you through His eyes:
Perfect, free, and happy
 playing by Jesus' side.

Carolyn Harney
Copyright © 1984
Used with permission.

Perhaps the greatest surprise in our ministry is the physical and emotional healing which can happen so deeply and quickly when we pray for miscarried, aborted and stillborn babies. For example, after praying for her three traumatic miscarriages, Sandy returned home to find her seven year old son, who had been hyperactive since birth, able to sleep through the whole night for the first time and behave normally in school the next day. During the next weeks Sandy found that not only was her son's hyperactivity gone, but also his learning disabilities, which had been diagnosed as permanent, disappeared. Another example is Jan, who wept uncontrollably as she prayed for her sister's aborted child, whom she had promised to keep secret from her parents. After this prayer Jan was able to conceive children, even though during the three years since the abortion she had suffered progressive deterioration of her reproductive organs and was told that she would never be able to conceive.

Almost every family can benefit, as did Sandy and Jan's families, from praying for miscarriages, abortions and stillbirths because these losses are so common. Approximately ten to twenty percent of all pregnancies end in miscarriage (not counting the fifty percent of fertilized eggs which are never implanted).[1] There are currently more than one and a half million abortions in the United States each year (four abortions for every ten live births),[2] and two stillbirths for every one hundred live births.[3] Babies are the group of people who are most overlooked in our prayers for the deceased.

How do we know we can pray for these babies, and how do we know they need our prayers? At times we've been taught that we can't pray for them because they are in limbo. At other times we've been taught that they don't need our prayers because they are in heaven.

## Are Babies Sent to Limbo?

St. Augustine sought to oppose the teaching of Pelagius, who denied our need for God to transform us in order for us to experience new life in Christ. Augustine's most powerful argument was the Church's practice of insisting on the baptism of infants. Augustine concluded, very reluctantly, that unbaptized infants must be damned, although to the mildest degree of punishment.[4] Later theologians, such as St. Thomas Aquinas, argued that the unbaptized child was not personally guilty and therefore not deserving of punishment.[5] Some suggested that there might be another place for unbaptized babies which was neither heaven, hell nor purgatory. A popular tradition grew up by which such innocent but unbaptized babies were sent to a place called "limbo," where they did not suffer the pains of hell but could not experience the fullness of God's love either. Limbo was thought of as a state of natural happiness which excluded heaven and the beatific vision.[6]

Although the Roman Catholic Church has never condemned discussions of limbo, neither has it ever affirmed the existence of such a place.[7] According to the research of modern theologians such as Monika Hellwig, the whole idea of limbo arose out of a theological misunderstanding:

> The ordinary catechisms and religious instruction have sometimes given a wrong impression as to what limbo was about. The word "limbus" (of which the dative and ablative in Latin are "limbo") means "the margin or periphery." As far as can be discovered, the original discussion was about what happened to

infants who died unbaptized before they had made any moral decisions. The original answer of theologians was, in effect, "We will have to place the question in *the margin* because we simply do not know." Apparently, by some confusion, it came to be understood that it was the infants and not the question that was in the margin ("limbo"). Then the "margin" became a special place on the other side of death. It's commonly understood in those terms, and has been taught as catechism in those terms. The traditional teaching was simple, "We don't know. But we do know that God is merciful."[8]

Modern theology emphasizes a God who is merciful, and it also emphasizes the role of the Christian community in bringing a child into the life of Christ. Much scriptural evidence supports our growing view of God as a merciful healer rather than a harsh judge and has led us to see purgatory as more like a hospital than a prison (see Chapter 5). Since evidence supports believing that God mercifully opens heaven to the unbaptized patriarchs of the Old Testament (1 Pet 3:19; 4:6) and to unbaptized martyrs (e.g., the feast of the Holy Innocents, which claims heaven for the unbaptized children murdered by Herod), how can we assume that heaven is closed to unbaptized babies? Both Scripture (e.g., 1 Tim 2:4; Rom 8:32; Acts 17:25–28) and Vatican II speak of God's desire to save all people.[9] If God desires to save all people, there must be a real chance of salvation for each one—something not provided by the limbo theory. Today theologians speak of a "baptism of desire," whereby a person may choose God when the normal means of sacramental baptism is not available. Baptism of desire means desiring to be incorporated into Jesus as fully as happens through sacramental baptism. Although a baby does not ordinarily have the decision-making ability of an adult, some theologians suggest that the child is given this ability at the moment of death. Others propose that a baptism of desire may be supplied by the parents of the child or even through the prayers of the whole Church. The story of St. Perpetua's prayers for her deceased, unbaptized brother Dinocrates (see Chapter 3) is an example from Christian tradition of how the grace of baptism can be mediated to a deceased child through the prayers of a family member. [10]

Today we see baptism for infants in the context of the love of parents and the Christian community, who are committed to bringing the child into Jesus' life, rather than emphasizing baptism as an isolated means of saving infants from limbo. If parents and the Christian community can help choose baptism for a child before its death, why cannot parents and the Christian community help choose baptism for a child after its death? Even when belief in limbo was strong, the Church recommended trusting the providence of God and invoking the prayer of the Christian community in a Mass of the Angels for deceased babies. Today the Roman Catholic Missal includes "Funeral Mass of a Child Who Died Before Baptism." Thus parents of children who die without baptism are told that "they can entrust the final lot of their child to the mysterious but infinitely kind and powerful love of God, to whose grace no limit is set by the earthly circumstances which he in his providence has allowed to come about." [11]

A deceptively simple statement of the issue comes from Daniel Poling, an Anglican theologian, who said of unbaptized babies, "Of course they will be saved. If they are not saved, I don't want to be either." [12] St. Thomas Aquinas tells us that our very desire to pray for a person is a movement of the Spirit within us and a sign that God wishes to save that person. [13] Perhaps all the evidence we need that babies reach heaven is that our hearts cry out in unison with Daniel Poling and with Jesus, who said, "Let the children come to me and do not hinder them; for to such belongs the kingdom of heaven" (Mt 19:14).

## Babies Need Healing

While some have believed that we could not pray for babies because they were in limbo, others have believed that they did not need our prayers because they were resting comfortably in heaven. But often when we begin praying for unborn children we see or sense them being filled with light and becoming more and more healed. Can an unborn child need healing? The findings of prenatal research and Christian tradition support our belief that unborn children can die in need of healing. If babies can die in need of healing, then they are also in need of our love and forgiveness offered through Jesus in prayer rather than limbo's isolation from prayer and Jesus. We pray for a baby because its wounds long for a deeper touch of Jesus' love and a reconciliation with those who wounded it. If we are correct in seeing the next life as a state of healing and ongoing growth (see Chapter 5), then babies too must need healing of the hurts they have already suffered in this life, hurts which would keep them from fully giving and receiving love in heaven.

## Prenatal Research: Hurts and Memories

How do we know that babies need healing? Prenatal research has shown that babies in the womb can see,[14] hear,[15] taste,[16] feel pain,[17] dream,[18] and cry.[19] Research also indicates that babies can remember and suggests that memory may even be present at the moment of conception. At one time medical science taught that a child could not remember before the age

of two because his central nervous system was still too immature. This view began to change in 1948, when David Spelt
proved that a fetus could learn a conditioned response to a loud
noise and remember it for up to three weeks.[20] Today there are
several theories to explain how a fetus can remember, perhaps
even from conception. Karl Pribram's theory is that memory
depends on protein molecules in the single cell rather than on
complex neural connections,[21] and Lyall Watson's theory is
that memory is stored in a spiritual body that accompanies our
physical body.[22]

One of the most dramatic illustrations of memory in the
womb is the work of psychotherapist Dr. Andrew Feldmar.
He had three patients who tried to kill themselves at the same
time each year. The dates seemed meaningless until Dr. Feldmar realized that each of these patients was attempting suicide
at a time which would be the anniversary of their second or
third month in the womb. When he investigated their histories, he discovered that the dates of the suicide attempts were
the dates when each one's mother had attempted an abortion.
Not only was the timing of each patient's suicide attempt reminiscent of an abortion attempt, but even the method was similar. One patient whose mother had tried to abort him with a
darning needle tried suicide with a razor blade. Another,
whose mother had used chemicals, tried suicide with a drug
overdose. When Dr. Feldmar's patients realized that their suicidal ideas were really memories of their mothers' attempts to
kill them, they were freed from the compulsion to commit suicide.[23]

Dr. Frank Lake, founder of the Clinical Theology movement in England (similar to pastoral counseling in the United
States), devoted much of his life to treating people like Dr.
Feldmar's patients, who suffered from the effects of traumatic
prenatal and birth memories. After working with thousands of
patients, he came to believe that most severe personality dis-

orders (psychoses) could be traced to prenatal trauma, especially from conception through the first three months in the womb.[24] Other psychotherapists such as R.D. Laing, David Cheek and D.S. Winnicott agree that the level of distress experienced by a fetus can be as great as the agony of an adult who will commit suicide rather than remember.[25] The intensity of a baby's distress can be this great precisely because its memories are so primitive. One psychiatrist speaks of fetal memory as " 'gut-level' remembering," because the fetus has only powerful impressions with no ability to sort them out, thus making them especially "intense, diffuse and pervasive."[26]

What kinds of things do babies remember? Because the life of the child in the womb is so intimately connected with the life of its mother, the child's memories are connected with its mother's experiences and reactions. This relationship can be understood physiologically as based upon hormonal and chemical transfer across the placenta. Every emotion we feel produces hormonal and chemical changes in our bloodstream. When a pregnant woman feels fear, anger, joy, peace, etc., the changes in her blood chemistry are shared with her child.[27] There may also be psychic communication between mother and child whereby they can pick up each other's thoughts, in the same mysterious way that any two people who are close may know what each other is thinking. In his book *Secret Life of the Unborn Child*, Dr. Thomas Verny gives examples of women who, shortly before their miscarriages, were warned in dreams by their babies that they were about to miscarry.[28]

Just how quickly mother and child can share feelings is demonstrated by an experiment in which pregnant women were told that their babies weren't moving. Each woman became alarmed that something was wrong with her baby, and within seconds the baby (observed through ultra sound) was kicking—apparently in response to its mother's fear.[29]

When a child is exposed to stress in its mother for even a short time, the child will demonstrate an increased activity level lasting for several hours.[30] What happens to a child who is exposed to stress in its mother for a long period of time? The fetus whose mother is exposed to severe prolonged stress has an increased activity rate up to ten times as great, and when the period of emotional disturbance lasts for weeks, the hourly averages of fetal movement are greatly increased during the entire period.[31] The effect on the child may be so great as to even take its life; there is a higher incidence of stillbirth among women who suffer extreme stress during pregnancy (e.g., having no husband and no family support).[32] If children of highly stressed mothers are born, they tend to be irritable and hyperactive and have low birth weight, disturbed gastrointestinal function and sleeping and feeding problems.[33] These are the babies that doctors and parents call "difficult" babies. The symptoms persist into childhood, and "difficult" hyperactive babies become "difficult" hyperactive children.

Dr. D.H. Stott has done the most long-term research to date on the lasting effects of prenatal stress. He found a direct one-to-one correlation between certain kinds of stresses in the mother during pregnancy and later physical and emotional problems in the child. The kind of stress that had the greatest negative effect was prolonged tension in the marriage relationship. The effects of physical illness, accidents or even deaths of relatives could not compare with the effects of prolonged marital discord.[34] In his study of over thirteen hundred children and their families, Dr. Stott found that a woman in a tension-filled marriage runs a two hundred and thirty-seven percent greater risk of bearing a child with physical and emotional problems than a woman in a loving relationship.[35] An example that confirms Dr. Stott's research is that of a seventeen year old mother who was coerced by her parents into marrying the father of her child, and then found herself living with an alcoholic wife-batterer. She left her husband, but he kept trying to force her to return and even threw a brick through her window. Her child vomited fresh blood and died twenty hours after birth. An autopsy revealed three peptic ulcers.[36]

Fortunately, babies can pick up and remember love and enjoyment as well as trauma. For example, Boris Brott is a symphony conductor who was able to play the cello line from certain pieces of music which he had never seen before, as if he already knew the score. He learned from his cellist mother that these were pieces of music which she had played while pregnant with him.[37] Recent scientific research confirms that the fetus not only hears and responds to music, but interacts with it and can distinguish between various kinds of music.[38] The love of parents is the single most important thing that children pick up in the womb, and it can overcome the negative effects of many stresses and traumas.[39] Dr. Franz Veldman, a Dutch scientist who developed "haptonomy," the science of touch, teaches parents to make loving contact with their unborn child. A mother (or father) can communicate with a fetus from the age of four and a half months by placing her hands on her womb. If she sends her love especially through the right hand, the child will begin to move to the right side of her womb and curl up with its neck under her right hand. If she then sends her love through her left hand, the child will move to the other side and curl up under her left hand. In this way she can rock the child back and forth. If she does this at the same time each day and then misses her "visit" with the child one day, the child will begin to kick, as if protesting even this momentary loss of loving communication which it has learned to expect.[40]

## Christian Tradition

Christian tradition knows that babies in the womb can pick up both hurts and love. The meaning of the doctrine of original sin, according to St. Thomas Aquinas, is that each of us suffers from the effects of sin because from the moment of conception each of us has been hurt by being exposed to less than perfect love.[41] Perhaps this is why many Christian groups include a prayer for exorcism in the ritual of baptism, asking that the child be freed from any evil it has already encountered during its nine months in the womb.

Our tradition acknowledges shared joy as well as sin, as we recall that the first two people to recognize Jesus were Elizabeth and John, the child in Elizabeth's womb who shared her joy (Lk 1:39). Mary's three month visit to Elizabeth was in keeping with the traditions of biblical society, where a pregnant woman would leave her husband and her other responsibilities and go to the home of a friend or relative who could provide seclusion. During her time away, she would pray, read Scripture and focus her thoughts on God in order to give her child a beautifully formed soul.[42]

Eastern Orthodox Metropolitan Anthony of Surozh speaks for many Christian traditions when he says:

> There is a limit to communion in words, but there is no limit to communication in other ways. Ultimately, a meeting between a soul and God takes place at the heart of silence. A meeting between two persons takes place beyond words. It takes place where God is. And in the Orthodox Church we insist that when a woman is pregnant she should make her confession, put all her life right, receive Communion, pray: because the relatedness there is between

her and the child is such that what happens to her
happens to the child.[43]

These words are very beautiful, but perhaps as you read
you are thinking of your own deceased or living children and
feeling guilt or fear. Perhaps you are a mother who was under
severe stress during pregnancy, or a father who wasn't ready
to be a father when your child was conceived. Perhaps you are
thinking of the hurts your children suffered because you aren't
perfect. If so, then the most important thing to say about how
babies can be hurt is how they can be healed.

Barbara Shlemon tells the story of a baby who was pro-
foundly hurt in the womb and who was healed. When Barbara
met seven month old Jennifer, she was still at her birth weight
of six pounds. Doctors said that Jennifer was the most retarded
child they had ever seen and recommended putting her in an
institution. Barbara learned from Jennifer's mother that she
had had three previous miscarriages and expected to lose Jennifer also. The mother was so certain this would happen that
she raised all her defenses against giving life to Jennifer so that
she would not have to go through losing her. She communicated to Jennifer, "Don't come to life because we can't handle
losing you." When Jennifer was born, she was literally unable
to receive life and could not assimilate any nourishment. Barbara prayed for the hurts Jennifer experienced in the womb,
asking Jesus to be with her in the womb and call her to life by
telling her she was wanted and would be cared for. Within
three weeks after this prayer, Jennifer was up to the normal
weight for an eight month old, and at the age of eighteen
months she was learning to speak and to walk.

Babies in the womb can pick up and remember love, and
they can pick up and remember hurts. Jennifer lived to be
born, and loving prayers healed the hurts she suffered in the
womb. (Parents can always ask Jesus, who transcends time, to

heal the hurts which they or their children may have received in the womb or in later life.) If Jennifer had died like her miscarried siblings, she would still have needed healing of her hurts and she could have received it through loving prayers. Just as the child can receive love in the womb, so it can continue to receive love after death.

## Mothers Need Healing

Jennifer's mother could not give love to Jennifer because she needed healing of the hurt of previous miscarriages. Doctors and hospitals have often treated miscarriage as if it were no more serious than a cold, fixed up by a brief medical procedure. Family members and friends have often told mothers, "Don't worry—you can always have another one," as if the dead child were an anonymous piece of tissue rather than a unique person. But when mothers and other family members do not grieve for miscarried, aborted and stillborn babies, they are often left with the kind of crippling pain felt by Jennifer's mother.

At one time we thought that a parent would grieve much less (if at all) for a baby than for someone with whom they had a longer relationship. But recent studies have found that parents who have just lost a baby show emotional and physical grief reactions similar to those seen following the death of any loved person.[44] Furthermore, there is no significant difference in intensity of grief for a miscarriage, stillbirth or death of a newborn. Even in early miscarriage, before "quickening," intense grieving occurs.[45] Larry Peppers and Ronald Knapp, authors of the first study to compare grief for miscarriages, stillbirths and neonatal deaths, conclude:

> Our data provide direct evidence of prenatal attachment. Apparently the affectional ties develop very

early in pregnancy. The suggestion that grief or mourning is proportionate to the closeness of the relationship leads many people to assume that the quality of a relationship is also associated with the length of time invested in it. Our data suggest that this is not the case, that the intensity of grief is as great in miscarriage as it is with the loss of a neonate.[46]

Dr. Peppers and Dr. Knapp went on to write *Motherhood and Mourning*, a more complete study of forty-two grieving mothers.[47] They found that all of the mothers mourned with equal intensity, regardless of the kind of loss they had experienced. Intense mourning usually lasted four to six months after the loss, with continued mourning for another six months or more. Typical stages of grief included shock, disorganization, anger, guilt, loss and loneliness, relief and reestablishment. This and other studies show that many women never move through these stages and develop psychiatric problems ranging from chronic depression requiring hospitalization to "shadow grief," a constant ache or emotional dullness in which a person cannot fully respond to the present moment.[48]

Why is grief for babies so intense and long-lasting? Studies suggest three reasons:[49]

(1) Lack of community support or encouragement for the expression of grief. Family and friends often try to avoid discussing the death and encourage the mother to forget about it, and there is often no funeral service or other established means of mourning.

(2) There is usually no concrete image of the child to say goodbye to. One woman said of her stillbirth:

When a child is born dead, there is nothing. The world remembers nothing, and the gap in the womb is replaced by an emptiness in your arms . . . you are not recording a birth or a death, but both at once. It is the ultimate contradiction—I felt I had created death.[50]

(3) Suddenness and unpredictability of the death leaves the mother with anger and guilt because so much has been left unsaid and undone. For example, one grieving mother felt so much guilt over the death of her baby that she went to the police six months later and confessed to killing her child. Although innocent, she was tried for murder and saved from conviction only by an attorney who understood the guilt of grieving mothers and arranged a psychiatric evaluation.[51]

Doctors and others who have become sensitive to these factors in the loss of a baby have developed many ways to help parents—for example:

• allowing parents to see and touch the baby, no matter how early the miscarriage or how damaged the stillborn. One hospital found that there were no pathological reactions in mothers who touched their newborns prior to death;[52]

• encouraging parents to name and baptize the child and to arrange a simple funeral;

• encouraging expression of grief feelings;

• parents' support groups and groups aimed at preventing similar deaths.* One grieving couple started the Michigan Leu-

---

*Miscarriage support groups now exist in most areas in the country. For information, write AMEND, c/o Maureen Connolly, 4324 Berrywick Terr., St. Louis, Mo. 63128.

kemia Foundation to fight the disease which took their child. They invited other grieving couples to join them, and of the one hundred and fifty couples who have worked with the organization since 1952, there has been only one divorce.[53]

The secular literature describes many such caring efforts to help parents work through their grief at losing a child, with an emphasis on accepting the loss. What is missing is what we find heals grief most deeply: knowing that we can have an ongoing relationship with a deceased loved one and that we can enter into this relationship with Jesus any time we pray.

### Power of Prayer To Heal Intense Grief

When praying with a woman who has lost a child, it is important to let Jesus' love touch the circumstances which cause intense and long-lasting grief. We do this by:

(1) encouraging her to share her heart with Jesus by expressing her grief and other feelings about the death and all the circumstances related to it;

(2) inviting her to ask Jesus to give her the child to hold and appreciate with him;

(3) letting her, with Jesus, say and do all the things for the child she wishes she had said and done. Asking her to tell Jesus all the ways she wants to continue to relate to the child through him in the future.

What follows are excerpts from a letter in which Elizabeth describes how she experienced these three steps in praying for her stillborn child.

(1) Elizabeth shares her heart with Jesus by expressing her grief and other feelings about the death and the circumstances surrounding it.

> I cried and cried. I asked Jesus what we needed to do. He said, "Forgive." I wondered who. I struggled and searched, I questioned and cried. Finally I realized whom I was angry at: God the Father. I don't mess around with any flunkie—I go right to the top.
>
> I yelled my anger at my Father. How could he take my baby? He responded that it was his child; he had numbered its days and designed its life.
>
> Then I recalled the anguish I felt when the elevator stopped at the maternity ward by mistake rather than at the operating room where the dead fetus within me was to be removed. Remembering this, I screamed, "Why did you do this to me?" He said, "Trust me." I couldn't trust him. But I did trust Jesus. With Jesus' help that evening I was finally able to forgive the Father.

(2) Elizabeth asks Jesus to give her the child to hold and appreciate with him.

> I felt as though I held him in my heart. A little boy. A first-born son. Jesus told me that I could select a name for him and then he would baptize him.

(3) Elizabeth with Jesus says and does all the things for the child she wishes she had said and done.

> I named him Michael. I felt as though I held him in my heart as I told him how much I loved him and

missed him and longed to meet him. Then miracu-
lously Jesus baptized him.*

Although Elizabeth's prayer included many of the common healing elements in praying for unborn babies (e.g., forgiving God, baptizing the child), other such prayers might
focus more on asking forgiveness from the child or forgiving a
doctor (see complete prayer at end of chapter). Possibly Elizabeth's next prayer would focus on telling Michael the ways
she needs him as a powerful intercessor and asking Jesus to
show her how she and Michael can continue to give and receive
love with each other *through Jesus.*

Elizabeth's letter closes with a description of how this
prayer healed her so she could love God, herself and others
more.

The biggest release came in my love for the Father.
The loosening of anger from my heart, mind and
spirit freed me to receive more of his love. That love
flooded me with a depth of joy I had never experienced before. I was also freer to love myself as a
woman, having released the disgust I had felt at hav-

---

*In asking Jesus to baptize a deceased infant, we are asking Jesus to do whatever
still needs to be done for that infant whether it be initiating baptism of desire or re-
newing it with a deeper celebration of Jesus' love offered through us. Ideally, as recommended by the Council of Trent, this prayer should be completed by a Eucharist
in which we receive Communion and join Jesus praying for us and the deceased to
draw closer to him forever. The Eucharist is also an ideal time to give Jesus' love to
others who may have been forgotten, such as the thirty-five hundred children aborted
daily in the United States. Especially at the Eucharist the deceased are empowered
with Christ's total forgiveness on Calvary. By receiving Christ's forgiveness for themselves and then extending that forgiveness toward all who have hurt them, the deceased are enabled to enter heaven, the state of loving the whole mystical body of
Christ forever.

ing carried death inside me. But what especially grew
was my love for my two living children. I no longer
resented them for being alive. I hadn't even realized
that I had resented them—but a part of me did. The
Father blessed me additionally the next year by using
me to lead two other women to this kind of release.
One woman had had an abortion, the other a stillbirth.

Elizabeth had initially recognized her need for healing because after her stillborn her marriage ended in divorce. Ninety
percent of bereaved couples are in serious marital difficulty
within months after the loss of their child.[54] Marital difficulties
arise primarily because of the inability to share grief. Whenever possible, we try to pray with both the mother and the father, and have found that shared prayer for healing grief can
not only heal both parents but also strengthen their marriage.

## Grief for Unwanted Children

Among those who read the rough draft for this chapter
were several women who have had miscarriages. When one of
them, Karen, read the following section which compares grief
for miscarriages with grief for induced abortions, she burst out
angrily, "How can you compare me with a woman who *chose*
to kill her baby?" Karen had deeply wanted a child and blamed
herself for her miscarriage. She felt guilty for those moments
of her pregnancy when she had resented the discomfort of
morning sickness or feared the changes that a child would
bring in her marriage. Karen's angry reaction at being compared with women who didn't want their babies and chose to
abort them could have been for many reasons, including even
her anger at herself for the few moments when she hadn't
wanted her own child.

Like Karen, every pregnant woman has ambivalent feelings about the baby who will cause her several months of physical discomfort and who will change her entire life in unknown ways. Occasional feelings of not wanting one's child are not enough to cause a miscarriage. The reasons for miscarriage are complex, ranging from conscious rejection on the part of the mother and failure to care for her pregnant body, to emotional hurts which limit her ability to nourish a new life, to physiological factors such as those fetuses which are deformed beyond hope of survival. Nevertheless, a woman who basically wants her child and miscarries may feel guilt and self-doubt as she recalls every moment of her pregnancy when she was not a "perfect" expectant mother. An extreme example of such guilt is the grieving mother described earlier in this chapter who turned herself in to the police for murder. Although distorted, such guilt may really be a sign of how much a woman basically loved and wanted her child.

Just as women who basically want their babies may have ambivalent feelings during pregnancy, so women who do not consciously want their babies also have ambivalent feelings. So often, as in the case of Jennifer's mother, a woman does not consciously want her child only because unhealed hurts have overshadowed her feelings of love. Despite their feelings of rejecting their child, such women also grieve if the child is lost through miscarriage or stillbirth, and they may feel especially great guilt leading to anguish and despair.[55] Many women who have chosen abortion have later reported that even as they lay on the operating table they told their child, "I'm sorry. Forgive me." Terry Selby finds that twenty-five percent of his therapy patients who have had abortions and who relive the abortion experience in therapy will begin to shake and cry out, aware that they are reliving the death agony of their child which they had empathically sensed even as the abortion was taking place.[56]

Our experience in inner healing prayer confirms that women who choose to abort a child grieve for their babies. We have often prayed with women who, many years after an abortion, still struggled with unresolved grief. Grief for an aborted child may remain buried and unresolved because of the depth of guilt attached to it. Although women who miscarry and women who choose to abort may both have ambivalent feelings, the woman who aborts her child is different from the woman who miscarries in that she has to deal with the fact that she has been actively involved in taking the life of another human being. We can never know all the inner and outer pressures leading to her action and so we cannot judge her, but such a woman often subconsciously fears judgment so much that she cannot bear to face her feelings of guilt. We have prayed with women who were still struggling with unresolved guilt and grief over abortions they had as long as fifty years ago. Only when these women asked for and received forgiveness from their dead child and from Jesus were they freed from the torture of guilt.

Yet when I (Sheila) did a research project on the psychological and spiritual effects of abortion, I was puzzled to find that most studies claim there is little or no negative effect. Such studies are usually based on questionnaire surveys of women who have had abortions. Then I found an article by Dr. Ian Kent and his colleagues, who had felt the same puzzlement. Dr. Kent had observed fifty women who gave a variety of reasons for entering psychotherapy, none related to abortion. After a long period of therapy, when they had developed a deep trust relationship with the therapist, they revealed a previous abortion and began to express feelings of mourning, love, regret and identification with their aborted child. Dr. Kent wondered about the discrepancy between his own observations and the many studies claiming little or no negative effects of abortion. He and his colleagues designed a typical questionnaire survey and did a study of seventy-two women—and got the same results as other such studies: little or no negative effects. The results showed a general absence of affect, with little intense emotion reported. But in examining the data more closely, he concluded that the very absence of affect was really emotional numbness, a significant negative effect in itself. Dr. Kent believes that the hurt of abortion is so deep that it is repressed and will rarely be revealed outside of a deep trust relationship.[57]

Several other studies have appeared which confirm Dr. Kent's work and find chronic guilt, anniversary depression, psychosomatic illness, drug and alcohol abuse, suicide attempts, psychotic breakdowns and other symptoms in women who have had abortions.[58] The Ohio Regional Director of Suiciders Anonymous reports that out of the four thousand women with whom the group had contact during a thirty-five month period, eighteen hundred or forty-five percent of the women had had abortions.[59] The problem of guilt over abortion is also found in other cultures. The *Wall Street Journal* reported recently that Japanese women who had abortions thirty or forty years ago are increasingly going to Buddhist temples where they pay $115 for a ritualized service to get rid of their guilt for the abortion, experienced in recurring bad dreams. The service includes the dedication of small statues to the aborted babies.[60]

Guilt over abortion is a theme of an essay by psychiatrist Dr. Arthur Kornhaber, in which he gives the case histories of patients who aborted their babies and felt more or less guilt and grief depending on how spiritually and emotionally developed they were. The two who were the least developed spiritually and emotionally felt little conscious guilt or grief. The two women who were more developed spiritually and emotionally struggled with guilt and grief; one eventually killed herself.[61]

Perhaps the work of Dr. Kent and Dr. Kornhaber explains why women who have had abortions and who come to know Jesus so often ask for healing prayer. In a deep trust relationship with Jesus and with other Christians they can begin to uncover and share their feelings, and as their inner life develops, so does an awareness of the wound of abortion. An abortion is such a deep wound that even the cells of the body remember it when the conscious mind has forgotten.

I learned this when I prayed with Martha. Martha's pastor and I had been praying with her about her troubled eighteen year old daughter Susan. Susan had frequent violent outbursts toward family members. Nothing seemed to help Martha or Susan until one day when I showed Martha some material on praying for aborted babies. The next day Martha came to us with something she had never shared before: she had had an abortion before Susan was born, and then she had tried to abort Susan. During the twenty-three years since her abortion she had not been aware of any negative effects and had virtually forgotten about it. Martha asked for the sacrament of reconciliation, and then we participated in a Mass of the Resurrection for the dead child and for any part of Susan which had died in the abortion attempt. During the Mass, Martha's back began to hurt. The pain moved to her stomach, and just at the time of consecration she collapsed on the floor. For the next twenty minutes, Martha experienced the whole process of delivering a child. Her body went through the contractions of labor, and she told us that she felt as if her forehead were soaking wet and as if there was blood all over her. We prayed for Martha, inviting her to give her baby to Jesus and Mary to be cared for. When the pains ended, Martha was able to stand up and resume the liturgy. The next day Martha told us that her chronic back pain was gone for the first time in years. She said, "I feel really good inside now, as though a burden has been lifted, as though it's finally out. I can breathe now. I can talk." Martha's grief for her aborted child had been buried so deeply that even she no longer consciously knew it existed. During the months that followed, Martha's daughter Susan gradually improved. It seems likely that Susan's violent outbursts were expressing the trauma of the abortion locked in Martha's back, because after the Eucharist, not only did Martha's back remain healed but Susan's violent outbursts ceased. Susan began relating to family members in more loving ways than ever before.

If I had been able to continue praying with Martha, I would have asked Jesus to heal whatever hurts in Martha had caused her to abort her child. Many studies indicate that not only does the loss of a baby through miscarriage, abortion or stillbirth need healing, but the loss itself may be a symptom of a previous hurt.[62] In Dr. Kent's study of women who had had abortions related earlier in this chapter, he found that in most cases these women had rejecting mothers who unconsciously or even consciously wished to abort them. Dr. Kent believes that his patients' abortions of their own babies were a form of symbolic suicide. Having turned their mothers' rejection against themselves, they now wished to destroy themselves.[63] In another, unpublished study of forty of his women patients with a history of abortion, therapist Terry Selby found that seventy-five percent of them had been sexually abused as children, fifty percent had been physically abused, and fifty percent had experienced the death of a parent, spouse or other significant person for whom they had not grieved.[64]

Although I was not able to follow up with Martha for healing of the hurts underlying her abortion, I *was* able to follow up with Diane, another woman who suffered the after-effects of abortion. Diane had had an abortion when she was seventeen, nine years before she came to us. She was so traumatized by the abortion that she spent several months in a mental hospital, and during the next nine years she engaged in frequent self-destructive behavior such as drug abuse and suicide attempts. When Diane first came for prayer, she brought her new baby, Sarah, whom she was considering giving away for adoption because she could not believe that any child would want her as a mother. As Dennis prayed with Diane, she experienced unconditional forgiveness from her aborted child and a deep exchange of love between them. After the prayer, much of Diane's self-hatred was gone. She felt worthy to be a mother, and she decided to keep Sarah.*

I followed up with Diane and learned more about her early life as I continued to pray with her. Diane's mother, Jane, had lost her beloved father while she was pregnant with Diane. Jane spent the rest of the pregnancy in deep grief and full of anger at relatives and at her husband, who would not take her to see her father before his death. When Diane was born, the umbilical cord was wrapped around her neck and both she and Jane nearly died. Throughout Diane's childhood she had terrifying dreams of drowning; the dreams ceased when she began taking drugs at the age of sixteen. Diane was both physically and sexually abused during childhood.

When the hurt of Diane's abortion was healed, all of these other hurts surfaced. Her guilt over her abortion had been an inner blockage, preventing God's love from reaching any part of her. As we prayed for her earlier hurts, Diane came to see her abortion as only a symptom of how she had felt so hurt that she had come to hate life itself. Fifteen months after our first prayer with Diane and after several sessions of follow-up

---

*This prayer is recorded on a thirty minute videotape, as Tape #12 of our series *Praying with Another for Healing*. The videotape is called "Prayer with Diane for Healing Abortion" and is also available on audio tape. For information on where to order, see Appendix E.

prayer, she told us, "I no longer have to fake that I am happy. I no longer have to fill my emptiness with drugs and alcohol. I feel real peace for the first time in my life."

Women like Martha, her daughter Susan and Diane are not the only ones who carry unhealed grief over an abortion. *Men and Abortion*, by sociologists Arthur Shostak, Gary McLouth and Lynn Seng, contains the results of their study of the effects of abortion on one thousand men. They conclude: "Abortion is a great, unrecognized trauma for males, perhaps the only one that most men go through without help." During the abortion experience, although these men might have appeared cold as they tried to fulfill our society's expectation that men remain in control, most of them felt isolation, grief, guilt, anger at themselves and their partners, recurring thoughts and dreams of the child, and fear of physical and emotional damage to the women. As one man said, "It's a wound you cannot see or feel, but it exists." Although the authors of *Men and Abortion* take a pro-choice position on abortion, they recommend post-abortion counseling to help men mourn the loss of their child.[65]

## Family Members Need Healing

When a child dies, not only mothers and fathers but the whole family is affected. In my experience with Martha, the hurt over her dead child which Martha had buried was picked up and lived out by Susan, her living child. In his book *Healing the Family Tree*, Dr. Kenneth McAll describes his work of healing the living by praying for a deceased family member, often a miscarried, aborted or stillborn baby.[66] Dr. McAll believes that a dead child who has not been lovingly accepted by its family and committed to God will cry out for love and prayer to a living family member, often a twin, the next child in the family or the most sensitive person in the family. When the dead child is loved, grieved for and committed to God (especially through a Mass of the Resurrection), the living person is freed. Among his patients Dr. McAll has treated two hundred and five women with anorexia nervosa, a disease in which the patient refuses to eat normally and may starve to death. In eighty-four percent of these cases, there was an ungrieved death in the family tree: sixty-two percent of the deaths were babies, twenty percent were war deaths, and twelve percent were suicides. When the deceased person was grieved for and lovingly committed to God, the symptoms of anorexia ceased. Dr. William Wilson, a psychiatrist at Duke University, has had similar experience with one hundred percent of twelve anorexic patients.[67] Anorexia has many causes,[68] but one factor may be an unconscious wish not to live and give life to more children because of an ungrieved death in the family.

We believe that Dr. McAll sees an important truth, from the point of view of the dead child. When we deny our eternal relationship with any deceased member of our family, something tugs at us from the next world asking to be recognized. In *The Ambivalence of Abortion*, Linda Bird Francke's words are reminiscent of Dr. McAll as she describes a "little ghost" who appears unbidden since her abortion.

> I have this little ghost now. A very little ghost that only appears when I'm seeing something beautiful, like the full moon on the ocean last weekend. And the baby waves at me and I wave at the baby. "Of course we have room," I cry to the ghost, "of course we do."[69]

While Dr. McAll and Linda Bird Francke may be teaching us something about the impact of the deceased child as it tries to contact living family members, there are also many reasons from the point of view of the living to explain their need for healing—reasons which complement rather than contradict Dr. McAll's work. For example, in the case of surviving brothers and sisters of a deceased baby, one reason the next child after a death may need healing is that grieving and bonding are two very different processes which cannot easily be carried out at the same time. Parents like Elizabeth, who have not finished grieving for a deceased child, will not be able to bond deeply with the next child.[70] Sometimes this may be a way of protecting oneself against future hurt, as in the case of Jennifer's mother who couldn't let herself love Jennifer because she couldn't bear to lose another loved baby. Also, during a subsequent pregnancy, women are often anxious and fearful and this is communicated to the child. They may continue to be overanxious and protective mothers after their child is born.[71]

Children who have already been born are also affected by the death of a baby. Parents often think that children are unaware of their mother's pregnancy, but even young children know when their mother is pregnant and they know if she has a miscarriage or an abortion.[72] When Matt's brother John died (see Chapter 2), Matt experienced symptoms that are typical of the surviving child—for example, anger at doctors, hospitals and God, guilt and resulting self-punishment, disturbances in cognitive functioning and school performance, depression and sadness. Girls may also experience fears of childbearing and womanhood because of identification with the mother.[73] The symptoms of mourning in parents, such as shock and depression, can be terrifying to a young child. One study found that even infants two to four months old are seriously disturbed and depressed when their mothers sit in front of them mute and without facial response for two or three minutes.[74] Children may feel abandoned by their grieving parents, and parents may put up an emotional barrier to their living children because of guilt and loss of confidence in their parenting ability.[75]

Bereaved children may also feel confused because they are grieving differently than their parents. A child younger than four usually understands death as only a temporary separation. Children aged five or six often believe that the dead can see and hear but simply can't move. Between seven and nine children begin to understand death as an irreversible, final state. At this stage a child may dream more about death and begin to look at his own death. Between ten and twelve death is accepted as universal, irreversible and inevitable. Grief during the teenage years is marked by missing a certain caring relationship.[76] Because children grow in awareness of the meaning and finality of death, they usually do not grieve intensely immediately after a death but are more likely to grieve intermittently for years to come.[77] Eventually children work through three main questions:

Did I cause it? (Children believe that wishes have power, and if a child has ever wished that a person wasn't around and then that person dies, the child may feel responsible.)

Will it happen to those I love?

Will it happen to me soon?

At every age, children need assurance that they have done nothing to make this person die and that they are loved even when their grieving parents cannot be emotionally present to them. Bereaved children may signal their need for loving help by repeated aggressive or hostile behavior, a prolonged drop in school performance, or regressive and insecure behaviors that persist over time.[78]

When parents work through grief for a miscarried, aborted or stillborn child, they are freed to offer loving help to their living children. When they give and receive forgiveness with their child, they no longer carry guilt and anger or transfer it onto other family members. Prayer for a lost baby can heal living children and entire families, as in the case of Sue.

Sue had six miscarriages and two living children, four year old
Julie and two year old Jason. During a retreat, Sue attended a
Mass of the Resurrection at which she was invited to pray for
deceased loved ones. Sue prayed for her grandmother, with
whom she had lived in early childhood. At the end of the Mass,
when she was invited to let Jesus bring into her heart whom-
ever he wished, Sue was surprised to have the following experience:

> I saw in my spirit six joyful children run into my
> arms. I just stood there thinking "Whom am I going
> to hug first?" and it felt as though I embraced them
> all with my heart. I knew they were my kids, and I
> especially rejoiced to see how much the youngest one
> was loved by the others. The children radiated love,
> to Jesus, to me, and to one another. This was the first
> time I had "seen" them, but I had, and still have, the
> feeling that they know me quite well.

The next day, Sue and a friend prayed together for Sue's six
miscarried children. They symbolically baptized all of the children and gave them names. Sue describes the changes she saw
in her family when she returned home:

> Before the retreat, Julie seemed like a fragile flower.
> She was very sensitive and cried easily. She accepted
> Jason but she was very annoyed by him. She had six
> little dolls (the same number as my miscarriages) that
> she was very attached to. Each had a name and each
> had to be accounted for at all times. She seemed to
> feel responsible for them and anxious about them.[79]
> Since my return, her attachment to those dolls be-
> came considerably less. Now they are toys that she
> enjoys playing with, but she doesn't worry about

them. She is curious, lively, happy, less serious and much less sensitive. She plays with Jason more—she adores him and she's convinced that she'll marry him when they grow up.

When Jason was born, I was unable to bond with him, although I went through all of the motions. From the day Jason was born, every single day until I got back from the retreat, I would consciously and prayerfully say to him three times, "Jason, I love you." As I said this to my baby, I believed that God in his mercy would fill Jason with the love that I was lacking and trying so hard to feel. Still, Jason was almost hyperactive. He quit nursing when he was five months old and he didn't seem to care much for people. He wouldn't let me hold him for very long. When I got back from the retreat, I was filled to overflowing with love for Jason. Since my return, the change in his personality was almost immediate and has grown steadily. He has calmed down; he is much more people-oriented. He gives us big bear-hugs and wants to sit on my husband's or my lap. Jason seems to adore Julie too.

I also noticed an almost immediate effect on my sexual relationship with my husband. I really wanted my husband to know God's love for him, so I almost never said no. I would pray and ask God to help me be loving to my husband, but I guess all I was really doing was enduring it. Then, when I returned from the retreat, we both noticed that my frigidity had disappeared. My friends have told me that my husband is much more open and relaxed than ever before, and we're beginning to go out to dinner together and talk as friends rather than antagonists—something we've never done before in our marriage.

I'm getting to know myself all over again. A part
of me that wasn't there before is there now.

Perhaps the greatest healing of all was what happened to
Sue herself. Before the prayer for her miscarriages, she was not
able to recall any time in her life when she felt loved. Since the
prayer, she recalls many such moments. Sue had been suffering from "shadow grief" during all the years since her first miscarriage, and had never known it. Sue's shadow grief had been
a desperate way of keeping alive the memory of her six miscarried children. When Sue found another way to continue
loving those children, she was free to let go of her grief. We
find that the deepest healing of a miscarriage, abortion or stillborn comes when a woman experiences what Sue did at Mass:

This was the first time I had "seen" them, but I had,
and still have, the feeling that they know me quite
well.

If prayer for healing relationships with miscarried,
aborted and stillborn babies can bring healing to babies, healing to mothers and healing to whole families, how do we pray?

### Mother's or Father's Prayer for a Miscarried, Aborted or Stillborn Baby

Read Mark 10:13–16, where Jesus asks for the children to
come to him.

• *Forgiveness.* See Jesus and Mary\* holding the child and offering it to you. With them, hold the baby and ask forgive-

---

\*Our suggestion that Mary be included does not mean we regard her as having
equal stature with Jesus. All the events in Jesus' life described in the Gospels are living
events with healing power, which Jesus wants to share with us. When we include
Mary in this prayer, we are accepting Jesus' offer to share his experience of a perfectly
loving mother with whoever needs her (Jn 19:26–27).

ness from Jesus and from the child for any way in which you failed to love the child. (Catholics who have been involved in an abortion should also make use of the sacrament of reconciliation as part of this step of receiving forgiveness.) Then take a minute to see what Jesus or the child says or does in response to you. With Jesus and the child, forgive anyone else who may have hurt the child (doctors, other family members, etc.)—anyone who, even unknowingly, didn't nourish this new life. Perhaps you or another even experience anger at God for sending the child at the "wrong" time or for taking the child.

- *Baptizing into Jesus' Family.* Now choose a name for the child and let Jesus wash away all hurt by baptizing the child into his family. Say with Jesus, "I baptize you, (name), in the name of the Father and of the Son and of the Holy Spirit." Feel the water cleansing and making all things anew.

- *Prayer.* Say a prayer for the child to receive all the love that Jesus and Mary wish to give it. When you really want the child to be eternally happy even more than you want it to be alive again, place the child in the arms of Jesus and Mary and see them do all the things that you can't do. Close your prayer by asking that the child become a powerful intercessor for you and your family and by asking Jesus to show you and the child how you can continue to give and receive love with each other through him. Join with Jesus and your child in praying for your family.

- *Mass.* If you are Catholic, have a Mass said for the child and, if possible attend it or another Mass. As you receive Communion, let Jesus' love and forgiving blood flow through you to the child and to all other deceased members of your family tree.

## Chapter 8

# The Soul Lives Where It Loves

Death is the thing we fear most. We began this book with a study by Dr. Thomas Holmes, in which he found that the death of a spouse is the single most stressful thing that can happen to a person. The death of a spouse is the most stressful thing because the closer we are to a person, the more separation is associated with death. The most terrifying thing for a human being is to be separated from love, abandoned, cut off—and death seems to us the ultimate separation.

What can heal our fear of separation and death? In his study of one hundred and fifty people who have had near-death experiences (where they were considered medically dead but then revived), Dr. Raymond Moody found that a common element in these one hundred and fifty experiences was meeting/welcoming loved ones who had already died.[1] In another study of deathbed experiences (where people actually did die but were able to share what was happening to them in the moments before death), Drs. Osis and Haraldsson found that the most common element was a sense of joyful reunion with a deceased loved one.[2] People who have had such near-death and deathbed experiences almost always report that they no longer fear death. When our friend Bill was dying of cancer (see Chapter 4), he told us that the single thing which helped him most was "the people who are loving me from the other side." It is an assurance of connectedness that heals our fear of separation and death.

Connectedness not only heals our fear of our own death, but also our fear of the death of those we love. In Chapter 3 we spoke of the time we prayed with several people who were grieving a loved one. We had thought that the most helpful prayer would be for these people to find the strength through

Jesus to let go of their loved ones and accept the separation of death. But instead, as in the example of Kim, we found that the most helpful prayer was for them was to be assured by Jesus of their eternal connectedness to their loved ones. When this happened, they were easily able to accept the physical separation of death. When we have a sense of connectedness to those we love, we can move through any fear—even the fear of death.

A friend once shared with us the following story. Her husband had died a few years before, and she had a young son who was born just before his father's death. One day when her son was at a neighbor's house, she suddenly sensed her husband speaking to her. He seemed to be telling her that their son was drowning in a swimming pool. She ran next door to the neighbor's and found her son drowning in the pool, exactly as she sensed her husband telling her. She pulled her son out of the pool, just in time to save his life.

Why does this story move us so deeply? A story about a child's life being saved is certainly moving, but this story contains something more. A dead father is still there for his child, at the moment when he is needed most. Not only is a child's life saved, but death itself is overcome through the eternal connectedness of love. If such a thing can happen, then what have we to fear? The comfort contained in this story is the comfort Jesus wished to give us when he spoke the words his disciples most needed to hear after his death: "And know that I am with you always; yes, to the end of time" (Mt 28:20). Jesus promised us eternal connectedness to him and those we love through him. He knew we could not otherwise live out the commandment that precedes his promise and that he gave most often: "Do not be afraid" (Mt 28:10).

My deepest fear has always been abandonment and separation, that people would go away and never come back. I (Sheila) feared this until three years ago, when a beloved friend of mine died. My friend was Dr. Conrad (Koert) Baars, a Catholic psychiatrist and author. I first met him when I had been through a very painful experience. His friendship and love healed me to such an extent that I felt he literally brought me back to life. Koert believed that unconditional, affirming love was the foundation of all emotional health and happiness. Even as I was being healed through Koert's friendship, my mind was racing with answers to so many questions I had about how to help others. I worked for Koert, doing research and preparing manuscripts. Koert encouraged me as I incorporated his ideas into my own work with healing prayer, and he became a mentor as well as a friend. The gift I treasured most from Koert was the thing I needed most: I sensed that once Koert had committed himself to be my friend, he would never break that commitment, and my fear of abandonment began to leave.

On Sunday, November 19, 1981, I fell asleep with an especially great sense of peace and the thought that all—in both a personal and a cosmic sense—was well. On Tuesday I called Koert's home in Texas from my home in St. Louis to talk about a project we were planning together. Koert's daughter answered and told me that he had died—on Sunday. I felt shock and a wave of grief that was like being sick in my stomach. I called my spiritual director, who had also known Koert. He invited me over to his home a few blocks away, where we met in the chapel and cried together. When I left the sickness was gone from my stomach and I felt a strange mixture of sadness and joy. During the following weeks the joy intensified even as I continued to have tears of grief each time I thought of how I would not see Koert again in this life. Frequently during those weeks I would find myself singing a song I had heard only once, several years before. The words were:

> There's a river of life flowing out from me
> Makes the lame to walk and the blind to see

Opens prison doors, sets the captives free
There's a river of life flowing out from me.[3]

Each time I sang these words, I felt a sudden rush of joy and a sense of Koert's presence followed by an image. The image was of a door opening to heaven, through which Koert had gone, and of a great light—like a "river of life"—shining down on me. I had an awareness that death was completely different than I had thought. Instead of leaving, Koert was nearer to me than ever before, promising to help me in greater ways and empower me even more deeply to help others than when he was physically present. With that, deep roots of my fear of abandonment were pulled up; if death could not separate me from the presence of a person who truly loved me, then nothing else could either.

Why was I open to this experience of Koert's presence through the communion of saints, to the extent that it healed deep fears with me—rather than being devastated by Koert's death because of those very fears? The French philosopher Gabriel Marcel often wrote about ongoing relationship with the deceased as one aspect of the mystery of presence. Marcel understood "presence" as a shared life which is greater than the two who participate in it, an unseen reality which can exist between two people who are geographically distant just as it can be achingly absent between two people who are in the same room. To the extent that we are capable of authentic presence with our living loved ones, Marcel believed, so we will be capable of it with them after they have died.[4]

As a small child I was taught by loving grandparents to recognize the presence of God in nature, and I spent many hours gazing at trees or sitting by the ocean knowing that Someone was loving me through the waves and the sun. I think that these early experiences of presence to nature taught me how to listen and be truly present to a friend who was with me, and then how to know Koert's presence when he and I lived one thousand miles away from each other. Because I had learned to receive God's presence in nature and in friends both nearby and distant, by the time Koert died I had made room inside myself for his presence even from the other side of death. I knew that after his death, just as before, he was promising to help me and to empower me to help others.

In the three years since his death, I have found that Koert has kept his promise to help me and to empower me to help others. I have felt his help most clearly in my relationship with Matt and Dennis, whom I met through Koert. I had done a research project for Koert, for a book he wanted to write on the psychological and spiritual effects of abortion. As part of my research, he suggested that I write to Matt and Dennis to ask about their experience in praying at the Eucharist for aborted babies. Koert died before writing his book, and we have used some of the research I did for him in Chapter 7 of this book. After much correspondence, I finally met Matt and Dennis five days after Koert died. We felt an immediate resonance with each other, and our friendship and shared work began to evolve quickly.

A few weeks after we met, I experienced a crisis of self-doubt about what was evolving. I feared that I was not emotionally or spiritually mature enough to work closely with Matt and Dennis. I thought of some of the other women they had worked with, and I felt like a frightened little girl in comparison. My spiritual director and close friends encouraged me, but the turning point came one night in prayer. I sensed Jesus telling me that Koert was still a channel of his love for me and that I should ask Koert's help. I sensed Koert's presence, next to Jesus, and I asked Koert to intercede for me. That night I had a dream in which I was riding in a car on the way to Koert's house. We encountered several minor detours and delays which should have caused me to fear I would be late. But instead, as each delay came, I felt a calm assurance that I would still get to Koert's house at exactly the right time. When I woke up, my self-doubt was gone. I sensed the message of the dream to be that God trusted me with Matt and Dennis despite my areas of immaturity and would help me to grow so that I got where I needed to be at exactly the right time. During the three years since then, as my work and my relationship with Matt and Dennis have grown, there have been several moments where I wondered if I was ready for the next step. Each time I've sensed Koert's affirming presence, recalled the dream, and felt again a wave of calm assurance.

As well as helping me to grow personally, I have also experienced Koert continuing to teach me and empower me to help others. Shortly after Koert died, I was praying with a friend who had also been Koert's friend. As we prayed, I sensed that Koert was praying with us. I recalled how the air in Koert's office had always seemed almost thick with a kind of spiritual depth or presence, as if filled with many people who were loving Jesus. I sensed a whole philosophical and spiritual tradition which stood in back of Koert and which had nourished his understanding of how a person is born only through the gift of affirming love. I realized that just as Koert was continuing to help me from the other side of death, so many people had been helping him. He stood at the end of a long line of wise and loving people, each one inspired through the intercession of those who had gone before. I saw that when Koert committed himself to me, he had also extended to me all the sources that nourished him. I, too, now stood in the same current or channel of Jesus' love which had empowered Koert, and everyone who stood in back of Koert would stand in back of me also. After that prayer, I noticed a great difference in my ministry. I began to have a much more sure sense of which people were suffering from a lack of unconditional love, how serious the deprivation was and its particular quality within that person. When I prayed with a person, I would start by connecting myself with that special current of Jesus' love and wisdom which had empowered Koert, and ask not only Koert but all those who stood in back of him to intercede for the person. Since I have been praying for people in this way, I notice much deeper and more rapid healing in them.

Koert's death taught me that nothing can separate us from those Jesus has sent to love us, not even death. Not only was Koert still there for me, but he was there in the specific way I most needed him. Fr. George Maloney writes,

> All who believe in Jesus Christ are living members of his body and this presence to each member transcends the temporal and spatial limitations of their imperfect existence on this earth. Milton expresses this belief: "Millions of spiritual creatures walk the earth unseen, both when we wake and when we sleep." . . . Although your loved ones may not rival in holiness the great saints, still they are quite closely tied to you by God's gifting you with their love. The power of God still works in them, giving them a loyalty to you that impels them to help you with your every need, just as they wanted to do while they lived on this earth. If you take this ancient doctrine of the communion of saints seriously, you should be able to walk and talk with your departed loved ones. The love of God in them that still binds them closely to you becomes the powerful "wavelength" by which they can communicate with you. The greater your love for them, the greater the communication.[5]

I find that the more I open myself to the mystery of the communion of saints, by which Koert can continue to "walk and talk" with me even though he is no longer physically present,

the less I fear separation and abandonment in all areas of my
life. Knowing that I am eternally connected to loved ones
through Jesus heals my fear of living as well as my fear of
dying.

This mystery of eternal connectedness also stretches my
awareness of how I can extend the Lord's love to others in the
same way it has been extended to me. When I saw that not only
was Koert there for me, but also all those who had stood in
back of him, I felt as if I had been "grafted on" to his spiritual
heritage and had a share in everything that had been given to
him. I realized that when I love and pray for another, it is not
only I who love and pray but also all those who stand in back
of me.

For example, my friend Ann called me recently from her
home one thousand miles away to ask for prayer. Ann has always felt a sense of oppression, as if something dark was
weighing upon her, and an uncertainty that she was really
dwelling in God's light. She would become frightened whenever anything to do with the demonic was mentioned. Ann
learned that her Irish ancestors were druids who had practiced
witchcraft and human sacrifice. As soon as she discovered this,
she was certain that the weight of darkness she had always carried came from this heritage of witchcraft. Soon after her dis-
covery about her ancestry, Ann attended a retreat with a group
of others where she shared her awareness of some dynamics
within the group. One of the others in the group became frightened and angry at Ann's words and lashed out at Ann, accusing
her of being a witch—the very thing Ann feared most. Ann's
uncertainty that she belonged to God grew more intense, and
it was at this point that she called me to ask for prayer.

As I asked Jesus how I should pray for Ann, I became
aware of one of the strengths within my own spiritual heritage.
My ancestors are all Jewish, with an ancient tradition of mon-
otheism and an intense aversion to witchcraft. I have always

felt myself securely rooted in God and protected from any temptation to witchcraft or occultism. I sensed Jesus telling me that since I love Ann as a sister, I can share the strengths of my spiritual heritage with her. So I began my prayer for Ann by asking the intercession of all my ancestors who had a single-hearted love for God, beginning with Abraham. I asked that Ann be grafted onto my spiritual heritage in such a way that she share in all its strengths and be sheltered under its protection from witchcraft. I asked that Ann know as surely as I do that she is rooted in God and dwells in his light. I asked that Ann's ancestors be touched and healed of the hurts and ignorance that led them into witchcraft, and that they receive whatever they needed from my own ancestors. I also asked that both Ann and her ancestors be protected from anything negative in my heritage, and receive only what Jesus knew would give them life.

When I talked with Ann several weeks after this prayer, she told me all the changes she had experienced. The day after I prayed for her, she noticed that the sense of oppression she had always felt was lifting, and she felt a new security that she belonged to God. Since that day she frequently found the words "the one true God" going through her mind—words I had not used with her—and with these words a new interest and love for Judaism and Jewish people. Ann found a new hunger in her heart for the Eucharist as a place where she could be nourished by this "one true God," where before she had attended the Eucharist more because she thought she should. Ann's fear of the demonic disappeared as she felt a new confidence that darkness could not overtake her. She felt less threatened in the presence of the person who accused her of being allied with the demonic, and a few weeks later Ann spontaneously invited this person out to lunch. Ann works as a Christian psychotherapist and had always avoided praying with clients for deliverance because she was unsure of her right to confront the forces of darkness. Now Ann was able for the first time to pray for deliverance and found it a peaceful experience. Ann felt a new freedom to step out and use all her gifts of discernment because she now felt more securely rooted in God's protective light. When Ann told me all these changes, I felt that the Lord had answered my prayer by using a strength in my line of the Communion of Saints to bless Ann and redeem a weakness in her line.*

Just as a group of the deceased such as my ancestors could give life to one person like Ann, so one deceased person can give life to a whole community. We saw this when the three of us visited the Guatemalan village of Santiago Atitlan. Although the Guatemalan army has wiped out many neighboring towns of Indians, it avoids entanglement with the resisters of Santiago Atitlan. The poverty stricken Indians resist not with guns but with a martyr, Fr. Stan Roether. During his thirteen

---

*It is important to distinguish my openness to Koert and Ann's openness to my ancestors from the spiritualism spoken of in Chapter 3. The key question to ask in opening oneself to the influence of the deceased is whether such openness brings one closer to Jesus. Throughout both prayer experiences, I did several things that would help both Ann and myself grow closer to Jesus. First, I went to Jesus before going to anyone else and then allowed him to lead me, in one case to Koert and in the other to my ancestors. Second, I continued to focus on the departed only because I had an abiding sense of Jesus' presence. If I had opened myself to a deceased person who was not yet sufficiently healed to be a channel of Jesus' love, I would have noticed an increasing dissonance between my sense of that person's presence and my sense of Jesus' presence, a sign that the spirit in that person was probably not the spirit of Jesus. Third, in both cases the fruits of the prayers were greater love for self, God and others—a sign of Jesus' presence. If the beginning, middle and end of prayer all lead to a deeper hunger for Jesus, then the deceased are mediating Jesus' presence and love. If the prayer leads to anxiety, discouragement, lack of faith, hope or love, then the deceased are not mediating Jesus' presence and love but rather must be brought deeper into Jesus' healing love and forgiveness before they can become mediating intercessors. See also Appendix B, Part II in which Dr. Douglas Schoeninger compares criteria for healthy relationship with the deceased to those for a healthy relationship with any living person.

years as their pastor, he learned to speak the difficult Indian language fluently and taught the people new respect for their Indian heritage. He established schools and co-ops and worked for social justice, despite death threats from those wanting submissive Indians rather than Indians rising in dignity and seeking justice. Finally, on July 28, 1981, a para-military death squad killed Fr. Stan's body but not his vision. Although the authorities had forbidden all assemblies, the villagers rose in unison to expel the army.

When Fr. Stan's family asked that his body be flown back to the United States, the villagers complied but only after they made arrangements to keep his heart. They were also able to keep Fr. Stan's homemade coffin, since it did not meet airline specifications. So every year on his anniversary they again proclaim their freedom with a forbidden parade featuring Fr. Stan's empty coffin and cries of "He is risen." And every day when a villager needs Fr. Stan's courage, he goes to the village church to pray and touch Fr. Stan's heart enshrined there. What Fr. Stan could not accomplish with his life he accomplished with his death because those he loved took on his heart. Thus with Fr. Stan's risen courage in their hearts, the Indians of Santiago Atitlan continue the vision and the social projects for which Fr. Stan died.

When Stan Roether died, the people of Santiago Atitlan faced the same choice that Jesus' disciples faced: to live in fear behind locked doors or to be empowered by his Spirit. The Stan Roethers and our deceased loved ones who have lived as Jesus empower us through their spirit, just as the resurrected Jesus empowered his disciples by sending them his Spirit. Because Koert loves me, he continues to live with me from the other side of death and to share all that he has with me. Because I love Ann, I can live with her one thousand miles away, and share all that I have with her. Because Fr. Stan Roether loved the people of Santiago Atitlan, his courageous heart not only rests in the village church but also lives on inside each villager. As St. John of the Cross said, "The soul lives where it loves."[6]


### Prayer To Live with a Loved One Through the Communion of Saints

When St. Paul wrote his Letter to the Ephesians, he included a prayer that expressed his longing to live with "the saints" at Ephesus through the love that binds together the whole communion of saints:

> For this reason I bow my knees before the Father, from whom every family in heaven and on earth is named, that according to the riches of his glory he may grant you to be strengthened with might through his Spirit in the inner man, and that Christ may dwell in your hearts through faith; that you, being rooted and grounded in love, may have power to comprehend with all the saints what is the breadth and length and height and depth, and to know the love of Christ which surpasses knowledge, that you may be filled with all the fullness of God.
> Now to him who by the power at work within us is able to do far more abundantly than all that we ask or think, to him be glory in the church and in Christ Jesus to all generations, for ever and ever. Amen (Eph. 3:14–21).

Lord, show me which of my deceased loved ones kneels with you and St. Paul now before the Father and prays this prayer for me. Let me open my heart to receive its blessing as I join you and my loved one in praying this prayer.

Lord, show me all the ways you have already blessed me through my family line. Who needs to receive that blessing which is especially mine to give? Let all my ancestors who can mediate that blessing join me as I pray this prayer with you for the person who needs it most.

# I Am a God of the Living and Not of the Dead

To live so as to be always worthy of
God this surely is the *most certain way*
to be always with our dead.

There can be no doubt
that for their part
they have lost nothing
of their affection for us
*which deserved to live eternally.*

We may therefore be assured
that their desire for intimate union
with us, a union in a love perfectly true,
is *far greater* than even our own desire
for it. For they are *in God,*
the very Heart of Love.

But we may approach this Divine Love,
for it is *in God* "that we live,
and move and exist."
We also are *in God,* though not yet
so completely as they—God is *in us.*
But God is the heaven of faithful souls.
Heaven therefore is *in us*
in so far as God is there.
May we not conclude that our soul
is a sanctuary of the holy souls
as it is a temple of God?

Are we not justified
in thinking that we bear them
(after a fashion) in ourselves
and that they are *incomparably closer*
to our soul

than the little babe
of which she is the tabernacle
is close to its mother's heart?

Christ exceeded our most daring hopes
by making the mutual inhabitation
of the Divine Persons
the bond of our mutual intimacy
"That they may be one,
even as Thou and I are One."

There can be *no surer comfort*
than this active and sanctifying
communion
with our dear ones
in an intimacy *continually increasing*
as our *union* with God *becomes closer*.

God has *not* taken them from us;
He has hidden them in His Heart
that they may be *closer to ours*.

"God is not a God of the dead
but of the living."

From *The Splendor of the Liturgy*
by Maurice Zundel, published by
Sheed and Ward

# What About Hell?:
# How Can a Loving God Send
# Anyone There?
# (A Scriptural View)

Many people might read various Scripture passages about God's judgment and wonder if the vision that Hilda saw of God welcoming her son after his suicide (Ch. 5) has any truth or is merely wishful thinking. They may wonder this all the more when they find out that Robert, ever since his father corrected him in front of his buddies four years ago, had locked himself in his room. He constantly used abusive language, telling his mother, "You and God can both go to hell."

Many Scripture passages might suggest that a vengeful judgment awaits Robert. For instance, Matthew 5:22 tells us that abusive language such as Robert uses toward his mother makes Robert "liable to the fire of hell." Furthermore, Matthew 10:30 tells us that such abusive language toward God is reason to have Jesus disown us before his Father in heaven. And still other passages such as Matthew 6:15 say that unless Robert forgives his dad, "God the Father will not forgive your failings either." Can such vengeful statements about putting people in the fire of hell or about not forgiving be true statements about how God acts?

The question to ask is: When a lover is loving us the most, would he or she ever disown us, put us in hell, or not forgive us? Since God loves us at least as much as the person who loves us most, God would act at least as lovingly as the person who loves us most. To understand how God loves and what the above Scripture passages might mean for Robert, we have to hear the passages as they were spoken by a loving God using language which can only be properly understood by another lover.

## God Uses Lover's Language

Scripture passages cannot be understood until we understand lovers' language. Language regarding punishment is especially misunderstood. Punishment can more easily be understood when it is therapeutic, such as a mother telling her seemingly overtired child, "If you don't stop fussing, I'm going to have to send you to your room to nap." But what occurs when lovers threaten with vindictive punishment, or with punishment that is not therapeutic, such as God when he speaks of disowning us, putting us in hell, or not forgiving us?

Last month two of my friends helped me to understand what lovers like God mean when they use language which threatens a vindictive punishment. One friend, Terry, was patiently waiting for his three year old son James to put away his toys so that James could do what he enjoyed most, go on the weekly shopping trip with his dad. But James, anxious to leave, stopped with only half his toys picked up. Terry said, "James, if you don't pick up your toys, Daddy is going to have to leave you and that would break Daddy's heart." James, afraid of being left home alone, picked up the rest of the toys and a moment later was on his way shopping. Because Terry wanted so much to have his son James go with him, Terry had used separation language ("if you don't pick up your toys, Daddy is going to leave you") involving punishment (James being left home alone).

The other friend, Annette, used separation language involving punishment when she was trying to get her elderly father to move into her home. Once a month Annette traveled to visit her elderly senile father, only to find that his body was slowly deteriorating because of malnutrition. For months she had tried to convince her dad to move from the house in which he had lived for forty-seven years. But her dad never seemed to hear her plea until one day she said, "Dad, if you don't move out now, I'm not going to come back next month. I die every time I see you this way." Within a few minutes Annette's father had his bag packed. He was finally ready to give in to Annette's wish that he come and live in her home. Both Annette and Terry had used language involving vindictive punishment in order to tell someone they loved how much they wanted that person to be with them.

When lovers use vindictive punishment language, what sounds like a vindictive punishment (e.g., "I'm going to leave you at home" or "I'm not going to come back next month") is not at all a reliable indicator of what will happen. Terry would never have left his three year old son James alone; Annette had every intention of returning every month (she told me that she would have started going weekly if her father had not moved). The threatened vindictive punishment is given not because the person has any intention of carrying it out, but only to indicate how important it is to obey so that they can love each other more. So, too, God has no intention of carrying out his threatened punishments such as threatening to disown us, put us in hell against our will, or not forgive us. Rather, he threatens us so we will know how important it is to obey what he asks so that we can love each other more.

An example of such a vindictive threat would be Matthew 6:15. There Jesus tells us, "If you do not forgive others, your heavenly Father will not forgive you your failings either." He threatens to not forgive us only because Jesus wants to underline the importance of his command to forgive others, and not because he has any intention of withholding his forgiveness which is always given even before we repent. Forgiving others is important because when we carry unforgiveness toward anyone, all our relationships are affected and we are less open to giving and receiving love with God and others. Jesus wants us to forgive because he wants us to be close to him and those he sends to love us. Furthermore, withholding forgiveness would make God a hypocrite, as he is constantly telling us to forgive immediately and unconditionally. Threatened vindictive punishments (unlike therapeutic punishments) are not to be taken literally, just as we do not take literally what Terry said about his heart breaking if James hadn't picked up his toys, or we do not take literally what Annette said about herself dying each month when she saw her father deteriorating.[1] Not only vindictive punishments but also words such as "everlasting," "fire," and "hell" are not always to be taken literally but rather they are often intended as images. Although hell does exist as a possible state, we cannot understand this state unless we understand the images used to describe it.

The test to discover whether we are properly understanding a Scripture passage is to ask ourselves the question, "When someone who loves me is loving me the most, would he act in this way?" If so, we probably understand the passage. If not, we are probably making a mistake, such as taking something literally which is really intended as an image. Scripture is lovers' language and thus uses many images. Jesus spent a good part of his life trying to show the priests, scribes and Pharisees that the Scriptures spoke a lovers' language which they frequently misunderstood by interpreting it literally. So, for instance, Jesus constantly struggled with them as they literally interpreted the law and the vindictive punishments regarding such things as the sabbath observance or rules for cleanliness. Thus Jesus was always in trouble with them for such actions as healing on the sabbath or touching an unclean leper. Down through the centuries interpreting all of Scripture literally has led to many abuses, such as the imprisonment of Galileo or support for slavery.

Perhaps the time I (Dennis) saw the greatest abuse of reading all of Scripture literally was the day I was called to the jail to visit my friend Bill because he had just attempted to gouge out his own eye. By the time I reached Bill, the guards had chained his arms and placed him in solitary confinement because they thought he was crazy. Looking at his blood-stained shirt, I asked Bill why he had tried to gouge out his eye. He repeated to me Matthew 5:29, "And if your right eye should cause you to sin, tear it out and throw it away; for it will do you less harm to lose one part of you than to have your whole body thrown into hell." At the time I was struck by how crazy Bill had become by taking the first part of that passage, "and if your right eye should cause you to sin, tear it out and throw it away" so literally. But then I realized that I had spent the first twenty years of my life acting almost as crazily because I had taken the second part of that passage, that God would throw my whole body into hell, so literally. The truth of the matter is that the instruction to gouge out our eye is not to be taken any more literally than is the statement that God will throw our entire body into hell. Just exactly then what is Jesus saying in his lovers' language when he uses such images as "the fire of hell" or when he threatens such punishments as not forgiving us? In the afterlife story of the prodigal son, we can watch as God responds to the elder brother who is in the process of choosing between heaven and hell.

### The Elder Brother Can Choose Hell

If Scripture could put Robert in hell, it could also put the prodigal son's elder brother there. When Hilda told me the story of her suicidal son Robert and how for four years he had locked his door if his dad were present, and how he used abusive language with his mother, I felt her depression and discouragement. But Hilda's story is no more distressing or discouraging than the story Jesus tells us about the prodigal's elder brother. Although the elder brother describes himself as one who has faithfully served, Jesus describes him as being very unfaithful to the duties that Oriental culture assigns the eldest son. In fact, Jesus describes the elder brother as failing in many of the ways that Robert did.

Although the elder brother did not actually lock his door as Robert did, the elder brother did lock himself off from his father by going along with the prodigal's unthinkable crime of treating their father as if he were dead. One of the main duties the Talmud assigned the oldest son was that of being family reconciler. The Talmud would hold the elder brother responsible for any failure in communication such as that which happened when the prodigal asked for and was given his share of the estate. Not only the elder brother's refusal to be reconciler but also his active acceptance of his own share of the estate would have astounded the listener. But that is not all. As every Oriental knew, another main duty of the oldest son was to safeguard revered Oriental hospitality. At banquets he was expected to be the major domo, the one responsible for hospitality. Not only does the elder brother refuse to do this, but, worse yet, he argues with his father in public. Because of the father's authority, such an action was not just an affront to a person but it was also a crime against the culture, the religion and the family. Those who study Oriental culture tell us that the elder brother's public insult placed a "break in the relationship between the older son and his father that is nearly as radical as the break between the father and the younger son at the beginning of the parable."[2] In fact, experts in Middle Eastern culture point to a written record where a father who was insulted in public by his son followed the cultural expectation and killed his son.[3]

Jesus' Middle Eastern listeners could use the same Scripture passage that we used with Robert to suggest that a vengeful judgment awaits the elder brother. For instance, Matthew 5:22 tells us that abusive language such as the elder brother used toward his father makes the elder brother "liable to the fire of hell." Furthermore, Matthew 6:15 says that unless the elder brother is able to forgive the prodigal, God the Father will not forgive him either. We could go on with other passages about hell and punishment which might fit what the elder brother has done (e.g., Mt 8:12; 22:13; 25:41). But what do their threatened punishments mean when addressed to the elder brother?

Although we do not know whether or not the elder brother goes to the eternal banquet, let us suppose the worst. Let us suppose that the elder brother considered his father's action in welcoming the prodigal to be the last straw. Finally the elder brother speaks the truth to his father, "As far as I am concerned, I want nothing more to do with you or my brother, and that's final."

If the elder brother's choice really was final, he would find himself in the chaos which Jesus described through the image "everlasting fire of hell." What everlasting hell's chaos is like could probably best be described by whatever person at the prodigal's eternal banquet was considered the closest family friend. Such a family friend would remember the sleepless nights and anguish the father had as he searched each day for the return of his prodigal son. (Origen describes this anguish by saying that as long as a single person remains in hell, God remains on the cross.)[4] The family friend would also remember the way the father greeted the prodigal and perhaps most of all marvel at how the prodigal was now closer to his father than ever before. With this background the close family friend could grasp the chaos of hell, especially as he saw the elder brother refusing to come to the eternal banquet. If such a friend could yell at the elder brother, that friend would probably shout, "Don't you see the joy your father wants to share with you? You're crazy to refuse it! Look at how you're hurting yourself and your father and your brother each time you turn down their invitation to celebrate at the eternal banquet." But in eternal hell the elder brother will not change, but rather chooses the self-centered chaos within himself and projects that chaos onto even those who love him most. Thus eternal hell is Jesus' description for the suffering that happens inside the elder brother, others and God as the elder brother forever chooses himself.

Although the Church holds that it is a possibility that the elder brother could choose such a hell, the Church has never said that anyone has made such a choice or that anyone ever will.[5] How would we know if a person has chosen hell? Such a choice must be looked at from two viewpoints: the viewpoint of man and the viewpoint of God. In the parable of the rich young man, Jesus stresses how differently the possibility of salvation looks from man's viewpoint and from God's. When his disciples asked Jesus how anyone could be saved, Jesus said that from man's viewpoint it is impossible, but from God's viewpoint everything is possible (Mk 10:27). Piet Schoonenberg summarizes this parable when he says, "Hell is a possibility in us, and redemption is a still greater possibility in God."[6] When Hilda first thought about her son committing suicide, she thought of it only from the viewpoint of man. She thought that her son would surely go to hell until she saw the Father reaching out to her son and could consider the question from God's viewpoint. Similarly, the situation of the elder brother looks very different when looked at from the viewpoint of man and from the viewpoint of God.

### Hell from Man's Viewpoint

When the elder brother says to his father, "As far as I am concerned, I want nothing more to do with either you or my brother, and that's final," from his viewpoint he may well be choosing hell. Hell, from man's viewpoint, is the state of being stuck in one's self-centeredness to the extent of closing off any loving contact with God or anyone else. From this viewpoint, hell's stuckness is such that, left on his own, a person like the elder brother would remain in that stuckness forever.

From the viewpoint of the elder brother, he might describe his hell as follows:

> Hell is eternal. It is everlasting fire. It is irreversible. It is beyond man's freedom to change this decision. He can choose hell in this earthly life. His choice, as far as his human powers go to change it, is irrevocable. Hell is a most real possibility as man makes his choice in this life and it is everlasting frustration.[7]

Thus, from his point of view, the elder brother is probably correct in saying that he wants nothing more to do with his father and that his decision is final. But even though he may think so, the elder brother's "hell decision" is probably not final until God has given his input. Knowing the hurts and frustrations behind the elder brother's decision, the father chooses to honor that decision not by sending his son to hell, but rather by entering into that decision and healing the hurts that started the elder brother choosing hell.

## Hell from God's Viewpoint

Perhaps the most important thing to notice about the father's dealing with his eldest son is that he does not send his son away from afterlife's banquet. The elder brother can choose not to enter, and, by deciding to stay away from his father forever, can even start choosing hell. But the father does not judge with vengeance or impose hell on him as a punishment. By not forgiving we judge ourselves and can put ourself in a hell-like state. Until the elder brother forgives the prodigal and himself for being unfaithful, he will probably continue to feel judged.

God's judging wrath is usually a projection of our own anger against ourself. Outside the banquet hall, the father's action is trying to say to the elder son, "I love you and appreciate you; come on in." But the elder son interprets his father's action as saying, "I don't appreciate you. I am going to go inside and leave you."

When the father goes inside to the eternal banquet, the elder brother, who has not forgiven the prodigal, might find himself in a hell-like state and might imagine that the father is addressing the words of Matthew 6:15 to him: "If you do not forgive others, your heavenly Father will not forgive your failings either." But the truth is that the father has forgiven the elder son's unfaithfulness as the father tells his eldest son again that "all I have is yours" (Lk 15:31). That the father does not forgive (Mt 6:15) is not a statement of how God acts but a statement of how a person like the elder brother projects onto God what is inside of himself. If our anger is overreacting to another's "unfaithfulness," for example, to the point of not forgiving him, it is often because we can't forgive the "unfaithfulness" inside ourselves. Therefore, "the Father does not forgive you" not because he isn't offering forgiveness, but because we will not forgive ourselves and therefore are incapable of receiving the Father's forgiveness. Even the "unforgivable sin against the Holy Spirit" (the rejection of God's forgiveness given through the Holy Spirit) is only unforgivable because we do not accept God's offer of forgiveness (Mk 3:28).

The inability for someone like the elder brother to forgive himself usually comes from hurts. Perhaps the elder brother's deepest hurt might be described as abandonment (Lk 15:29). Because of the depth of that hurt, its roots may go back to the elder brother's childhood and the abandonment he felt after the sudden death of his mother. Or the roots of his hurt may go back to years of feeling abandoned by God as he struggled against insurmountable obstacles such as famine. The complaint he addresses to his father of feeling like a slave is probably just the tip of a deep iceberg of abandonment within. But for a person feeling abandonment at such depth, it would be very difficult to love and forgive himself because he usually cannot do that unless he first takes in love (1 Jn 4:19). Thus it is not surprising that the elder brother who has felt abandoned continually "abandons" himself rather than face himself. Rather, for instance, than face his own unfaithfulness so that he can receive God's mercy and thus have mercy on himself, he clings to a false image of himself as being faithful (Lk 15:29).

Hurts, besides giving us a false image of ourselves, also give us a false image of God. Because of all the abandonment that the elder brother experienced in life, he is unable to go into the eternal banquet because he thinks that God has abandoned him. But until the elder brother's hurts are healed, he will be like the depressed disciples on the road to Emmaus who think they have become disenchanted with God, whereas in reality they have only become disenchanted with their false image of God as a political messiah (Lk 24:22). Since probably none of us live or die without hurts, all of us are like the elder brother in need of healing now and in afterlife.

## As Man Chooses Hell, God Chooses To Heal

If the person you loved most started choosing hell, what would you do? Although we may not be able to say with certainty what the Father will do when someone starts to choose hell, we do know that he will be at least as loving as the person who loves us most. What gives hope in considering the question of hell is that when a person starts to choose hell, the Father will choose to extend healing to that person. The Father has as many ways of extending that healing as he has of loving. Since the Father's ways of loving are infinite, the Father has an infinite number of scenarios to choose from as he extends his healing. Though the Father has an infinite number of scenarios to extend his healing, the following five short scenarios will give us a little of the infinite hope that the Father has for healing everyone, including the elder brother, as he starts to choose hell.

### First Scenario: Healing by the Father as Therapist

If, as we imagine, the elder son resists going into the eternal banquet and starts to choose hell, we do know that the father will seek him out in every possible way, just as any lover would do and just as the father did with the prodigal. The story of the prodigal son (especially Lk 15:25–32) describes one way in which the father, acting like a sensitive therapist, sought out his elder son. First, the father listened compassionately as the elder son got out all his angry feelings regarding the prodigal. In listening, the father did not condemn or vindictively blame the elder brother; he only promised to keep loving the elder brother even if he did not change. If the elder son continues to choose hell, perhaps the father's continued listening may allow the elder son to work through and heal the hurts that started the son toward that choice of hell.

### Second Scenario: Healing Through the Father Allowing Himself To Be Physically Beaten

Scripture scholar Kenneth Bailey has written his own ending to the prodigal story, in a play called "Two Sons Have I Not."[8] In the following conversation, Bailey suggests how the

Father comes to the conclusion that the only way to open his elder son's heart is to go out unprotected to his angry son even though he knows that his angry son will strike him.

Father:    Discipline will bring more rebellion. Forgiveness will change nothing. . . . If he strikes me, maybe then he will see his rebellion for what it really is.

Mayor:    But you must not do this. You may get hurt.

Father:    Will my suffering be any worse than that which I now endure? Is my heart at rest with him in rebellion far from me? I go, my friends.

A few minutes after the father leaves, the priest and the mayor hear the sound of a stick beating on a body. When the mayor asks the priest what will happen now to the elder son, the priest gives the following hopeful interpretation.

> I think he'll repent. For the first time he'll see that his pride really meant he secretly wanted the death of his father. He will be shocked at what he has done, especially when he finds that his father came to him on purpose, knowing what would happen. In a flash it will come to him that the stick should have been in his father's hand. He'll see that there's nothing he can do to make up for his actions. This will lead him to a broken-hearted repentance. Now he'll see something of the depth of his father's love. With rebellion burned out of him he will confess his unworthiness and repent. Don't you think so, O Mayor?

Whether we are as hopeful as the priest or not, what we do know is that the father will reach out in every possible way to heal his elder son. The creative possibilities of the father's love are beyond anything we can imagine, just as the death and resurrection of Jesus were beyond the imagination of the Jews who had waited for a Savior.

### Third Scenario: Healing Through the Cross of Jesus

The Anglican theologian and bishop, John A.T. Robinson, offers another possible scenario of how God might wear down the elder son's resistance by demonstrating his sacrificial love. Imagine that the elder son walks the road which eventually leads to hell.

> Somewhere along the first road, far or near from its beginning, man meets Someone, a figure stooping beneath the weight of the Cross. "Lord, why are you doing this?" each of us sometime or other asks. "For you, to prove that you are greatly loved by God." No man can indefinitely meet such great love, especially in his bitter emptiness and loneliness of self-love, and continue to resist. Man will not lose his choice to resist. He will want, like a feverish thirsting man on a desert, to stretch out to drink this life-giving water.[9]

Again, whether or not Robinson is right that neither the elder brother nor anyone else could finally resist such personalized love, what we do know is that Jesus will reach out in every possible way to heal. Although we and the Roman Catholic Church hold that it is a possibility to choose hell, Robinson shows how unlikely it is that anyone would ever actually make such a choice.

### Fourth Scenario: Healing Through Exorcism

What if the elder brother is too hurt, too sick to respond? Is there any way out of his misery? Such a person who is refusing God's love, which is life itself, seems to fit Dr. Yolles' description of a suicidal person, when Dr. Yolles says that only an unhealthy person can be driven to suicide. The Church too is discovering that suicide seldom, if ever, is a deliberate act (mortal sin) of cutting oneself off from God. As previously mentioned, the hurts which consume a suicidal person may lead him to jump out of a high window, not because he wants to cut himself off from God but because all the pressures in his life feel like flames in a burning building about to consume him. Since we can never know all the pressures that were in that suicidal person's life or in the life of the elder brother, we have no right to condemn. Just as we would intervene to stop a suicidal person, Jesus would probably also intervene to try to stop the elder brother's destructive behavior. Just what Jesus would do, we cannot say for certain. Perhaps in the severest case, Jesus might find himself praying a prayer of deliverance[10] or even of exorcism just as he did for the Gerasene demoniac (Mk 5:1–21). The demoniac had withdrawn by even "taking refuge among the tombs" and was so hurt and sick that he asked Jesus to leave him alone (Mk 5:7). Nothing, not even withdrawal or possession, need stop the healing power of Jesus if there is any openness to receive.

### Scenario Five:
### Healing Through the Communion of Saints

Through the communion of saints, Jesus and the Father also extend their healing to a person who starts to choose hell. The communion of saints is the name given to all people living and dead as they find themselves connected to one another by being connected to Jesus. For, "if one part is hurt, all parts are hurt with it;" (1 Cor 12:26). So, for example, all those at after-life's banquet belong to the communion of saints. Thus if there is something between the elder brother and the father, not only the prodigal but all those at afterlife's banquet hurt with the father. Those "saints" at afterlife's banquet grow in self-giving love and in their love for the father by reaching out to the elder son and all the broken ones, whether still on this earth or those who have died in need of healing.

Not only the saints in heaven but also the members of the communion of saints on earth can enter into the Father's love and into the infinite scenarios which offer undreamt of healing. For example, the story of Edward in Chapter 6 tells of a person released from a hell-like schizophrenia when others prayed for his ancestors. Whenever I see such a new and creative way of bringing healing to another, I am aware that I have just begun to enter into the infinite number of creative ways of healing extended by the Father, Jesus and all the saints as they reach out to offer healing to the deceased. During such an awareness, I begin to taste a little more the infinite hope that the Father and all the saints have for healing everyone, including those like the elder brother who have started to choose hell.

### Everlasting Fire of Hell:
### An Image of Healing

The infinite scenarios in which God chooses to extend his healing may well be part of what Scripture means by the "everlasting fire of hell." When Jesus speaks about the "everlasting fire of hell" he is using an image to describe the chaos of a person closed off from God. He uses this image to describe both the chaotic state of being permanently, completely closed off (dogmatically described as hell), and the state of being temporarily closed off (dogmatically described as purgatory). Many who have always thought of the "everlasting fire of hell" as referring to a permanent state may wonder how it can be temporary. The key lies in understanding the scriptural image of fire as well as the scriptural words for both "everlasting" (*aionios* in Greek) and for "hell" (*gehenna* in Hebrew).[11]

Jesus mentions "hell" or the Hebrew word gehenna seven times in the Gospel of Matthew, three times in Mark and once in Luke. Gehenna was a valley in southeastern Jerusalem regarded as accursed and associated with fire and death because pagans practiced child sacrifice at a shrine there. Thus Jesus used gehenna in speaking about hell because his Jewish listeners had already chosen gehenna as their image for speaking about a place of punishment for the souls of the wicked after death. When Jewish listeners such as the elder brother heard Jesus speak about the fires of gehenna or hell, it meant different things to different people. Although the fire was eternal, the punishment was not always eternal. For instance, the majority of Jesus' listeners who understood the Talmud and midrash set a limit of twelve months for all but the most wicked who not only sinned but also led others astray. Even condemned souls in gehenna could gain freedom through the intercession of the righteous and from recitation of prayers such as the Shema.[12]

Not only "hell" but also "everlasting" was understood by Jesus' listeners to be an image that could describe a temporary state. George Maloney writes: "Although writings of the Septuagint (such as the Book of Daniel and the Books of Maccabees) use words as 'forever,' 'eternal,' and 'everlasting' (*aionios* in Greek), the meaning is a popular description for an indefinite duration of a long period of time."[13] Thus "forever" or "everlasting" is an image and in no way is meant to be only "a metaphysical concept of unending, everlasting timelessness as we understand it today."[14] Karl Rahner agrees with Scripture

scholars such as J.L. McKenzie that when in speaking about
hell, Jesus used "everlasting" and such words as an image.[15]
Perhaps the most important thing to remember is not only that
words such as "everlasting" and "forever" are images, but that
they are images spoken by a lover. One day to a lover, such as
a father searching for his lost prodigal son or lost elder son,
could be "forever." After the loss of my granddad, my grandmother said that one day seemed longer to her than their previous fifty-two years of marriage. I remember a time when I
waited two hours for a phone call from someone with whom I
needed to be reconciled. Those two hours seemed like "forever." If the elder son made a final choice not to respond to his
father's healing initiatives, his suffering would be literally everlasting hell. On the other hand, Scripture's "everlasting hell"
could also be an image for whatever time it takes the elder son
to fully accept the father's healing, and thus can be an image
for what we describe as a temporary state of separation such as
purgatory.

Besides "hell" and "everlasting," "fire" is another image
used in the New Testament. "Fire" does not mean physical
flames which God created so that those suffering from the
flames might make expiatory payment to him for their sins.
God is not a vindictive judge but a healer. Thus fire is an image
of God's love which would be present even in hell. Even as the
elder brother, from his viewpoint, starts choosing hell, God's
love keeps inviting the elder brother to please come to the banquet. Such fire of the father's love is meant to purify, to burn
away at the elder brother's hardness of heart. It is the fire of
love that "torments." The more the father loves the prodigal or
the more the father loves the elder brother, the more such love
will "torment" the elder brother because it calls him to a different choice than the hell he is heading for. If anyone is in hell,
St. Isaac the Syrian tells us that even this person is not de-
prived of the love of God, but by his own choice experiences

as torment what those in heaven experience as joy.[16] Thus heaven, hell and purgatory are not different places, but rather different ways of responding to the fire of God's love. Heaven is being able to fully enjoy that love, purgatory is a healing process of opening oneself to that love, and hell is a final choice against that love. The only way out of the "tormenting fire" for the elder brother is to open himself to the father's healing love.

## God's Healing Love at the Moment of Death and Afterward

According to our Roman Catholic tradition, the basic choice for or against God must be made before death.[17] The elder brother would have to open himself to the Father's healing love before the moment of death, even though his openness might have to deepen considerably through the healing process of purgatory. Although our tradition believes that after death we cannot change our basic orientation for or against God, the Eastern Orthodox tradition holds that conversion can take place after death, until the last judgment.[18] John A.T. Robinson offers support for this tradition when he writes, "The New Testament never dogmatizes to the extent of saying that after death there is no further chance."[19] According to this viewpoint, even withdrawal or non-response to God after death might be part of the healing process. Withdrawal was part of the healing process in the story of the unrepentant prodigal who withdrew from God and had no intention of responding. If I were to write the ending of the prodigal story according to the Eastern Orthodox tradition, I might imagine the elder brother running away just as the prodigal did. Perhaps the way for the elder brother will be the way the prodigal was rescued from his hell-like existence. The unrepentant prodigal was locked into a hell-like existence that he could not change until he first experienced the love of his father who ran down the road and threw his reconciling arms around the prodigal's shoulders. Perhaps what will heal the elder son's hurts and prevent him from finally choosing hell will be what healed the hurts behind the prodigal's hell-like existence: a long period of withdrawal followed by the father's hug and the throwing of a party.

### Experiential Basis for God's Healing Love at Death

Besides Scripture, near-death experiences support our belief that God will offer love and healing before our final moment of death. Since Dr. Raymond Moody's *Life After Life* (1975),[20] there has been a growing acceptance that from twenty-one to fifty-nine percent of those who return from clinical death remember a near-death experience that is similar, despite varying religious and cultural backgrounds.[21] During a "life after life" near-death experience, a dying man may hear his doctor pronounce him dead while feeling himself sucked rapidly through a long, dark tunnel. He then finds himself outside his physical body looking down on the doctors still trying to resuscitate him. He experiences himself as having a spiritual body which is very different from his physical body, like a floating amorphous cloud that communicates by thought. Relatives and friends who have already died come to meet him and bring him to a "Being of Light" who accepts and loves him more deeply than he has ever experienced. (This group of relatives and friends is similar to our belief in the communion of saints, who through their love and prayer help us to move deeper into God's love.) Like a magnet drawn to iron, he is drawn to the personal acceptance and compassion of this dazzling Being of Light. Moody notes that although this is an experience of light, not one person doubted that it was a personal *Being* of Light.

Shortly after appearing, the Being of Light asks the question, "What have you done with your life to show me?" This question isn't accusing or threatening, but rather is pervaded with total love and acceptance, no matter what the answer. The non-judgmental Being of Light helps the dying person answer the question by presenting a panoramic review that is like a film of the individual's whole life. This review is meant to provoke reflection. The Being seems to know all and is displaying the review so that the dying person can understand two things: how he loved others and how he learned through his experiences and mistakes. Only when a person learns how he has loved, and how he can deepen his love, does the Being ask him if he would like to stay or return to earth. Although many would like to stay in the next world, all who have returned to tell of their experience have finally decided with the Being of Light that they still have a mission to fulfill on earth, such as raising their young children or giving others the total acceptance radiated by the Being of Light. Those who return from such experiences bring with them a new and enduring desire to love others and to grow in self-knowledge. They also have less fear of death because they have met an accepting God rather than the vindictive judge they expected. They did find the Being of Light's judgment but it was more the self-judgment experienced when a smiling, non-judgmental Mother Teresa of Calcutta awakens one to injustice in neglecting the destitute. Dr. Elisabeth Kübler-Ross reports that meeting such a non-judgmental God helps these people to continue to live non-judgmentally. For instance, a minister after returning from his near-death experience could no longer be minister of his church. He was enveloped in such a total love upon encountering the divine Being of Light that he could no longer teach condemnation in the way his denomination demanded.[22]

The Being of Light is much like the non-judgmental father

in the prodigal son story. Some, such as those who have attempted suicide, might have a distressful experience which Moody describes as being stuck and unable to approach the Being of Light (much as in our idea of purgatory). Maurice Rawlings, M.D. labels this as "hell," but then describes Jesus beckoning a thirteen year old youth out of this "hell," as could happen only in the temporary state of purgatory.[23] Dr. Kenneth Ring notes that if a person has had a distressful near-death experience and then clinically "dies" again, his second near-death experience is always a positive one.[24] Although Dr. Ring attributes the difference to a change in consciousness, a Christian might add that the change may also be from the healing flowing from the first experience. All near-death researchers admit that the meeting with the Being of Light is a widespread and healing experience.

Researchers are no longer arguing about the content of the experience, but rather asking why it occurs. Recent research, such as Dr. Ring's, rules out wishful thinking, psychological expectations, dreams or hallucinations, and pharmacological explanations for this transpersonal experience at death. None of these sufficiently explain why children often meet a deceased person they have never heard about, why some people have not just flashbacks but also flashforwards of future events, or how a hallucinating person could describe in detail every surgical procedure by those attempting to save his life.[25] Whatever the explanation, resuscitated people often remember a healing experience with a loving Being of Light offered before death's final moment. Thus it seems that there is experiential evidence for the view that before the final moment of death God is effectively healing in ways beyond anything experienced in life.

## Conclusion

What can we say about hell? We can say few things with certainty because God's ways are always beyond our ways. What we do know is that Jesus' description of hell (e.g., fire, everlasting, God vindictively sending a person there) is not a scientific statement or account about some future place or punishment. Rather, such a description is an image spoken by a lover who is trying to convey the chaos and destruction that happens when a person chooses to close himself off from God and others. Hell is not a vindictive punishment from God but our choice to refuse his healing love. "Everlasting fire of hell" (gehenna) in Scripture is an image frequently used to describe the chaos of being closed off, and is used for both the state of being partially closed off (dogmatically described as purgatory) and the state of being permanently or completely closed off (dogmatically described as hell). Neither Jesus, revelation, nor the Roman Catholic Church has ever stated that anyone has or ever will choose this dogmatic hell, but only that it is a possibility which could be eternally chosen before death.

All Christian theology is based on the Gospels, and "Gospel" means God's good news. Thus all Christian theology must be good news, even the doctrine of hell. As the three of us have written this chapter, we have struggled to see how the doctrine of hell could be good news and why the Church has preserved it as doctrine. What helps us most is to listen for the values which underlie the doctrine of hell and which the Church is trying to preserve. When we listen for the values underlying the mystery of hell, we hear God speaking to us about the mystery of the cross.

Only by looking at the cross can we understand the reality of man's freedom to reject God and the extent of God's saving love even for those rejecting his Son. The cross shows us that mortal sin is a real possibility—even some of those who were healed by Jesus could put him to death. Even those who knew the reality of Jesus' love and forgiveness from the cross could still choose to reject him. The cross reveals not only the reality of sin and our own possibilities for destructive behavior, but also the extent of what Jesus saved us from and how much we continue to need him as Savior.

But besides showing us the power of man to reject God, the cross also shows us the power of God to save man from the nightmare of sin. God will go to any extent to save us, even to sending his Son to die for us. Nothing, not even the worst rejection, can turn God away from offering us his forgiveness. If there is anyone in hell, that person is there by his own choice to refuse the deepest love offered forever. We are not to judge that anyone is in hell, but simply to pray with Jesus on the cross, offering his healing forgiveness and his paradise to the greatest sinner.

From man's viewpoint, we know that the greatest sinner could be like an unrepentant prodigal, stuck in self-centeredness and closed to God forever. But the process of choosing hell must be looked at not only from man's viewpoint but also from God's. As with the prodigal, our hope is in God's healing initiative. God's healing initiative to save all is central to the Gospel message:

And I—once I am lifted up from earth—will draw all men to myself" (Jn 12:32).

St. Paul's writings also include the hope that God will ultimately bring all his children home to himself (Rom 5:12–21; 11:30–32; 1 Cor 15:22, 28; Eph 1:10; 1 Tim 2:4; 4:10: cf. 1 Jn 2:2).

The final hope in the question of hell comes from God. Our hope comes from the fact that God loves us at least as much as the person who loves us most. And since God has so much love for each of us and perfect foreknowledge of our choices, we can surely hope that he would never create a person who would reject him by choosing hell forever.

# Non-Catholic Support for Praying for the Departed

## I. An Anglican View

A group of Anglican theologians reported to the Arch-bishops' Commission on Christian Doctrine how the living may pray for the dead, through Jesus Christ, that during the state of purification they may develop "a deepening of character and a greater maturity of personality."

Few people would feel that at death they were sufficiently mature for the direct vision of God or for his immediate presence; nor would they presume that engrained habits of sin could be immediately eradicated. To hold that any Christain, even the most faithful, will be transformed into immediate perfection at death seems to many people incredible and verging on magic. It would seem that the turning of a sinful person—even of a person who desired the consummation of the vision of God—into the divine likeness cannot be an instantaneous process if human nature and free will and the continuity of the individual personality across the divide of death are to be respected. In any case, since felicity as known in this life is temporal, and a temporal situation (at least as we know it here) is a context for action and development, how is it possible to picture a state after death in which such temporal characteristics as joy and felicity, though they are posited of persons, yet have no development? All these considerations make many Christians incline to the belief that development is possible after death; if this is so, then prayers

191

of intercession are in order. We could be forbidden to intercede only if the situation towards which our prayers were directed was unalterably static. Prayers for the development of the departed need not imply any doubt on our part as to the outcome of their further pilgrimage, as though they could be assured of salvation at the time of death and yet lose their way thereafter. They may rather be prayers for deepening of character and for a greater maturity of personality. Nor need prayers for light and peace imply a present lack. We may always pray for an increase (or even a continuance) of what is currently being enjoyed by the people for whom we pray.[1]

## II. A Presbyterian View

Douglas Schoeninger, Ph.D. is vice-president of the Institute of Christian Healing in Philadelphia and editor of the *Journal of Christian Healing* in which this article was first published.[2] Dr. Schoeninger writes from his experience as a practicing clinical psychologist specializing in family therapy and as a deacon in the Presbyterian Church.

### Thoughts on Praying for Departed "Loved-Ones"

Being of Protestant faith, I have been conflicted regarding the practice of praying for the dead. Is it a spiritually valid practice? As a psychotherapist working with families, I have witnessed the value of these prayers. Persons seem genuinely helped by praying for the forgiveness and healing of family members who have died.

Yet I am haunted by questions about this practice. One implication seems to be that prayers for the departed involve seeking contact and communication beyond the grave. In fact, prayers for the dead need not approach, in any way, contact with the dead. They are simply prayers to Jesus on behalf of the dead. Yet persons do experience, at times, the gift of presence and loving union or reconciliation with a departed love one for whom they are praying. I have experienced this myself especially in relation to a close friend who died recently.

In trying to make sense of these experiences of communion and reconciliation, and to deal with questions and concerns directed to me, the following thoughts have emerged. I offer these thoughts for your prayer, reflection and critique.

The Body of Christ is one, undivided. All true relationships are mediated by Jesus Christ and are part of one and the same Body. If these beliefs are true, then it would seem to follow that relationships would continue to grow and develop, in love, as part of the Body, beyond death. Otherwise, we would be saying that the Body of Christ is split into two unrelated Bodies, that Body which interrelates in this earthly life and that Body, the communion of saints, which interrelates in the next life. While there is a radical change in our state of being with death, a change which dramatically separates the living and the dead (those being transformed beyond the veil of death), there is no evidence in Scripture, that I have seen, that speaks of the Body of Christ as separated. There is one Body and therefore an ongoing relatedness, in Christ, within the Body, and in a special way among those He has called into a particularly intimate tie, eternally. Family ties, rooted in inheritance, are one such intimate collective within the Body of Christ.

Some fear any approach to a living relatedness between themselves and their deceased loved ones. They do not trust that such relatedness can avoid the temptation to resist mourning and to seek continued relationship apart from Christ. These dangers are real. All of us resist letting go of those persons, who are part of us, who have died. Thus, there is a danger in attempts to relate to and pray for the departed, a danger that stems from refusal to accept their death and trying to retain them in one's life as they were or apart from Christ's direction and mediation. Such attempts are made outside of Jesus Christ, who resides only in truth. These dangers sometimes conjure up images of mediums and seances wherein the spirits of the dead are called forth.

It has been a revelation to me that the dangers inherent in seeking communion with a departed soul are the same dangers in seeking communion, living relationship, with one yet alive in this life. Each of us struggles in every intimate relationship with a resistance to letting go of the other in their former ways of being. We must mourn that which is lost to us as the other grows and changes, in order to "let go" into receiving the truth of what the other is for us at present. Otherwise, we are living in false relationship, outside of Jesus Christ. Also, Christ is mediator of every true encounter. We almost instinctively seek Christ first, and His direction and mediation, if we are reaching out to touch one who is departed. Such is our fear of falling into apostasy and darkness. We must instinctively know that we cannot control our reaches beyond the grave, so great is the mystery and so limited our perception. Yet, how often do we recognize that the same depth of mystery and inability to control exist between oneself and another living person. To live in Christ I must no less seek Him to direct and mediate within and between myself and the living other than I would were I to become, in some sense, present to a departed loved one. The same possibilities exist for seeking relationship outside of Jesus, therefore, opening to evil influence and manipulation; the same possibilities exist for holding the other in bondage by refusing to let him or her be present to me as he or she "is." C.S. Lewis in *A Grief Observed* presents a very lucid account of his own grieving process after his wife's death. It is an account of working through the painful letting go of what had been. He documents his own attempts to "recapture" his wife as she was through remembrance and fantasy. These attempts turned in on themselves revealing their emptiness as he attempted to elevate memory to the level of the vitality of a living, present exchange. Having released his wife to be absent from him, into her renewed life apart from him, Lewis describes moments of experience in which he became conscious of his wife's presence, a totally different dimension of presence. This new relationship seemed at once "ungraspable" and, at the same time, deeper than ever before.

Such is also the experience of relationship in this life. Parents must let go of their adolescent children, a painful dying to hopes, expectations, images of success, past forms of intimacy, in order to receive the presence of the person within their child who is becoming now. It is in Christ whom I rest, in order to let go and risk a really fresh perception, and it is Christ who probes and knows the depths of the other and opens my eyes to the other being born now. This is no less true with those who live within material flesh than it is with those to whom I am tied by love in Christ, who have passed through the material barrier into the next form of life. In both cases it is one's refusal to yield negative patterns (e.g., resentments, dependencies, insecurities, unforgiveness of all kinds) and one's refusal to let the other grow and change (which is in fact an attempt to restrict the inward growing of Christ in them) that becomes an alliance with evil, an open door to manipulation by Satan and his minions. Christ will not empower, will not indwell, our attempts to keep another the same, which is a holding of them in bondage. Satan is author and co-conspirer of all such investment. Refusal to allow another to grow creates a home for Satan who eagerly awaits such opportunities to lend his hand to our insecurities and fears and unforgiveness by sending his minions to empower our fears, assure our rightness in unforgiveness and grant "sense" and authority to our assumptions

about the absolute absurdity of entrusting ourselves into an unknown, uncontrollable, untested, confusing future. While
there are special concerns with relating to those who have departed, the same kinds of dangers exist in time-bound relationships.

By restricting our relating to and prayer for the departed,
we sometimes fail to free ourselves and them through forgiveness, through releasing and freeing our love to flow to them
and through calling upon their love for us, calling upon their
intercessions before the throne of Grace on our behalf. When
we focus our attentions only on the dangers of being tempted
and misdirected in our relating to the departed, we, perhaps,
delude ourselves into believing that our earthbound relationships are not equally vulnerable to the same degree.

## III. A Jewish View

In Jewish tradition, the family of a deceased person prays
the ancient *Yizkor* or memorial service for the departed in the
synagogue four times a year and makes a charitable offering.
The following is a prayer from the *Yizkor* that might be said for
a deceased mother. Note the ways that this prayer assumes ongoing relationship with the mother, such as the request for her
forgiveness.

### In Memory of Mother[3]

Though we are separated, dear mother, in this sol-
emn hour, I call to mind the love and solicitude with
which you tended and watched over my childhood,
ever mindful of my welfare, and ever anxious for my
happiness. Many were the sacrifices you made to en-
noble my heart and instruct my mind. What I
achieved is because of your influence, and what I am,
I have become through you. Though you are no

longer physically present, the lessons that you imparted unto me shall ever remain with me.

If at times, I have failed in showing you the love and appreciation which you so worthily deserved, if I have been thoughtless and ungrateful, I ask to be forgiven. I pray that your spirit inspire me to noble and intelligent living, so that when my days on earth are ended, and I arrive at the Throne of Mercy, I shall be deemed worthy of you, and be reunited with you in God. Amen.

# Praying for Family Occult Involvement

The occult refers to practices which seek power or knowledge from sources contrary to God's teachings.

> Let there not be found among you anyone who immolates his son or daughter in the fire, nor a fortune-teller, soothsayer, charmer, diviner, or caster of spells, nor anyone who consults ghosts and spirits or seeks oracles from the dead (Dt 18:10–11).

Such practices can open a person to evil spirits and harm even the person's children to the third and fourth generations (Dt 5:6–10).

C.S. Lewis observes that we make the mistake of finding evil spirits everywhere or nowhere.[1] "The devil made me do it" is sometimes a lame excuse to flee responsibility or a lack of awareness that inner healing prayer is needed. But sometimes the demonic really is involved and occultism is one way of opening oneself to demonic influences. The influence of the demonic must be carefully discerned as Dr. Kenneth McAll notes.

> In 1964, Bishop Mortimer, then Bishop of Exeter, invited me to join the newly-formed Exeter Exorcism Commission. Although I had been in private psychiatric practice for only a year, I had twelve cases to present to the Commission because a number of doctors had referred to me patients who had been damaged by the occult.
>
> The Commission's work grew from that first

meeting, when only two Anglican bishops answered the invitation, to the present time when thirty-eight bishops are represented. Nowadays, every diocese in England has an appointed exorcist. The church is beginning to realize the dangers of the occult. But I do not want to exaggerate the prevalence of demonic involvement as this accounted for only four percent of the cases which I treated in hospital and outpatient clinics. The percentage of such cases now referred to me is rising, however, and my patients tend to be those who have failed to respond to other medical and psychiatric treatment. Many people, untouched by years of such treatment, have been cured by prayer, even when they had no knowledge that prayer was being offered on their behalf.

When there is a suspicion that occult forces are at work in a person's life, a prerequisite of any subsequent treatment is a thorough medical examination. Someone suspected of being under demonic control may in fact be suffering from depressive psychosis, schizophrenia or the effects of other organic psychoses. The person could be acutely neurotic; hidden aspects of his personality or an upsurge image from his unconscious could be the cause. Although all such diagnoses should be treated as psychiatric disorders, they do not exclude demonic control.

There may be illness that is solely mental; there may be mental illness together with demonic control; there may be demonic control alone. The test for this is not the presence or absence of mental illness but rather whether there is a response to prayer and to the Eucharist. This diagnosis should be as accurate as possible.[2]

Sometimes the demonic problem reveals itself in prayer. Our friend, Joann, was praying for Jesus to reveal the root of depression in her family. She and her prayer partner saw that eighty years ago a priest in their family line had had an illegitimate daughter. The mother's brother tried to kill the priest who hid for three months. Then he formally cursed the child and its descendants. Joann had never heard this story but her mother acknowledged that it was true. Joann's mother revealed the child was Joann's grandmother who was raised by the parents of the priest. Joann went to a Eucharist and at Communion with the blood of Jesus renounced the curse, broke it, and forgave both the priest and the one who cursed them. She asked for Jesus' blood within her to cleanse, heal and protect each generation. From that moment the depression in Joann, her mother, and her aunts vanished. Curses and other occult bondage are often real but Jesus is even more real and powerful.[3] As we pray for those family members involved in the occult or hurt by it, we can bond our family line to Jesus.

Praying for the deceased has power to bond not just our families but even whole nations to Jesus. Mae was a middle-aged woman who came to our friend Mary for prayer. For the last eighteen years since her mother's death, Mae despite years of therapy suffered from psychotic symptoms with five personalities. From October to March every year she could not get out of bed to do housework. Mae was suicidally depressed and lived in her own world with her head down, avoided all eye contact, did not receive touch, and answered only in monosyllables. Mary tried praying for inner healing of Mae's hurts but made no progress until arranging a Eucharist for Mae's deceased mother and Aztec ancestors.

At the Eucharist those praying had an image of Jesus gathering a vast crowd of Aztecs with heads lowered, who had in their ignorance practiced human sacrifice. During the Eucharist Jesus seemed to place his hands on each Aztec until that person understood that human sacrifices were wrong and repented. After each Aztec repented, he walked up a stairway to heaven. When the last Aztec climbed the stairway, Mae came out of her trance-like state for the first time in eighteen years. She began to speak normally and was able to look in Mary's eyes and allow herself to be touched. She communicated one consistent personality rather than five disintegrated ones.

Mary continued to pray with Mae during the next four months for the healing of other hurts behind Mae's depression. As her depression lifted, Mae began to dress herself, took over the kitchen, and now lives a normal life. Note that for Mae and most people, deliverance from occult influences needed followup ministry, especially inner healing of hurts. Often we ask that a person seeking deliverance prayer be accompanied by a friend who will provide such follow-up.

Follow-up after a deliverance from the occult should stress the power and love of Jesus Christ rather than the presence of demons everywhere. Deliverances are frequently followed by a period of temptation where the evil one tries to return by making a person doubt his new freedom. He may awaken in the middle of the night and again feel an evil presence or experience the same old temptation.

When these times of temptation come, a person can focus on the power of Jesus Christ and calmly assert it, knowing that the evil one has no more rights unless unhealed wounds or repeated sin invite Satan back. Although he may experience a desire toward an old temptation, he has new freedom to say "no" to it. The best way to maintain a deliverance from the evil one is to be delivered into the love of Jesus. The more a person is filled with the love and light of Jesus, the less the evil one can find a home in that person. When a person gives a home to the evil one through involvement with occult groups, it is usually because that person has experienced rejection and other hurts that have led to a desperate search for belonging. Follow-up ministry should thus include continued healing of deep hurts and association with a loving Christian community where the person can continue to be filled with Jesus' protective life, especially in the Eucharist.[4] Our book, *Deliverance Prayer*, provides further guidance for this ministry.[5]

# Blessing Places

For nearly two thousand years Christians have journeyed to the Holy Land to follow reverently in Jesus Christ's steps. Churches are erected wherever Jesus worked a miracle because there is a sense that the very place is sacred and a special place to pray for his actions to continue today. For centuries the Church has also blessed other places to be special places of Jesus' activity. The Church blesses everything from churches to ships and even fields on rogation days.

Places can not only be blessed but can also be desecrated. Desecration happens through occult actions or through an unloving death as when the blood of Cain desecrated the ground (Gen 4:10). Jesus often passed by the Jerusalem garbage dump, Gehenna in the valley of Hinnom, which pagans desecrated through the sacrifices of their children. This place could make a Jew unclean. Everyone acknowledged the evil there, so Gehenna became an image for hell (Mt 5:22). Today at Dachau where Jews were experimentally tortured and then fed to cremation ovens, a monastery of contemplative nuns prays for the victims and their persecutors that a desecrated place might become a sacred place of God's forgiveness and healing. When an unloving death has desecrated a place, then prayer for the deceased can make that place sacred.

In England a documentary by the BBC-TV showed how prayers for the deceased can change a place. Part of the documentary concerned Rev. Omand who regularly prayed at sites where there have been a number of inexplicable or unusual accidents. After he blessed the road and prayed for those who had accidents there, accidents stopped or declined. The place has been made sacred—protected by God and by the intercession of the deceased who have been brought to Jesus. In the course of research into this phenomenon for their documentary report, the BBC team investigated the accident prone stretch of road between Charmouth and Morcombelake in Dorset, on which there were neither dangerous corners nor hidden intersections. The Rev. Donald Omand blessed the road and prayed for those killed there to receive Jesus' healing love. The BBC team found that in the six months prior to Rev. Omand's prayer, there had been seventeen accidents on that part of the road and in the subsequent six months there was not a single accident.[1]

This practice of blessing a place or home has been repeated by others with similar results. One Christian counseling center found that blessing the room after each therapy session prevented the next client from picking up the fear, anger or other energy released by the preceding client. If a place or home feels in need of blessing, one should take three steps. First, minister to the living so that they are totally free to give and receive Jesus' love. Second, bless the place with holy water and the traditional blessing prayer or any prayer that focuses on how Jesus' love is overcoming all evil. Third, pray for the deceased who lived or died in that place that they might be filled with Jesus' life and join him in protecting that place. Extend this prayer to those who hurt or were hurt by the deceased. The ideal prayer setting is the Eucharist for the deceased, especially if celebrated in the home. This should end with praise and thanksgiving for God's presence.

## Blessing Disturbed Places[2]

### Blessing of a Home

P:    Our help is in the name of the Lord
All:  Who made heaven and earth

*P:*   The Lord be with you.
*All:*  May He also be with you

Let us pray.

God the Father Almighty, we fervently implore for the sake of this home and its occupants and possessions, that You may bless_____ and sanctify_____ them, enriching them by Your kindness in every way possible. Pour out on them, Lord, heavenly dew in good measure, as well as an abundance of earthly needs. Mercifully listen to their prayers, and grant that their desires be fulfilled. At our lowly coming be pleased to bless_____ this home, as You once were pleased to bless the home of Abraham, Isaac, and Jacob. Within these walls let your angels of light preside and stand watch over those who live here; through Christ our Lord.

*All:*  Amen.

The doorstep is sprinkled with holy water.

*Appendix E*

# Resource Materials

## Books

*Healing of Memories*, by Dennis and Matthew Linn (Ramsey, N.J.: Paulist, 1974). This brief book is a simple guide to inviting Jesus into our painful memories and letting him help us to forgive ourselves and others.

*Healing Life's Hurts*, by Dennis and Matthew Linn (Ramsey, N.J.: Paulist, 1978). This more thorough book helps the reader pray through hurts using the five stages of forgiveness to reach the final stage: gratitude for what has happened because of the new life that has come through it.

## Courses

*Prayer Course for Healing Life's Hurts*, by Dennis and Matthew Linn and Sheila Fabricant (Ramsey, N.J.: Paulist, 1983). The accompanying book can be read as a summary of ways to pray for personal healing or it can be used as a course of twenty-four lessons with journaling and prayer exercises to bring healing. For use as a course, there are twenty-four thirty-minute sessions available on video or audio tape.

*Praying with Another for Healing*, by Dennis and Matthew Linn and Sheila Fabricant (Ramsey, N.J.: Paulist, 1984). The accompanying book can be read as a guide to praying with Scripture, praying with another and the healing of grief (Theme 3, "Healing the Greatest Hurt"). If used as a course of twelve lessons, it is meant to follow the more basic *Prayer Course* and has twelve thirty-minute sessions available on video or audio tape. The present book, *Heal-*

215

*ing the Greatest Hurt*, may be used as supplementary reading for Theme 3 of *Praying with Another for Healing*.

*Dying To Live: Healing Through Jesus' Seven Last Words*, by Bill and Jean Carr and Dennis and Matthew Linn (Ramsey, N.J.: Paulist, 1983). In this set of eight thirty-minute sessions on audio or video tape, the speakers present a workshop on how the seven last words of Jesus empower us to fully live our remaining life time. The tapes may be used with the book upon which they are based, *Healing the Dying*, by Mary Jane, Dennis and Matthew Linn (Ramsey, N.J.: Paulist, 1979).

## Purchase of Above Books & Tapes

Paulist Press
997 Macarthur Blvd.
Mahwah, N.J. 07430
(201) 825-7300

## Rental of Videotapes (videotapes for courses may be rented in $1/2''$ VHS, on a donation basis)

Christian Video Rentals, 4453 McPherson, St. Louis, Mo. 63108, (314) 533-8423

## Additional Audio Tapes

A wide variety of audio tapes by the authors on prayer, healing and related topics is available from:
ALU, 504 Antioch Lane, Ballwin, Mo. 63011, (314) 227-7445

# Notes

## 1. Healing Through Grieving

1. Thomas Holmes and Richard Rahe, "The Social Readjustment Scale," *J. of Psychosomatic Research*, 11 (April 1967), 213–218. Recently British researchers also constructed a table of events that elderly people find most stressful. Again death of a spouse came first, followed by being put into an institution, the death of a close relative, major personal injury or disease, losing a job and finally divorce. Cf. John Nicholson, "Coping with the Seasons of Life," *World Press Review* (November 1980).

2. *Ibid.*

2a. Marian Osterweis, Fredric Solomon and Morris Greed (eds.), *Bereavement: Reactions, Consequences, and Care* (Washington, D.C.: National Academy Press, 1984), 20–41 and 284. Report of a study by the National Institute of Medicine.

3. O. Carl Simonton, Stephanie Matthews-Simonton and James Creighton, *Getting Well Again* (New York: J.P. Tarcher, 1978).

4. Alan Anderson, "How the Mind Heals," *Psychology Today*, Vol. 16, No. 12 (December 1982), 56.

5. Osterweis, Solomon and Green, *op. cit.*, 20–41 and 284.

6. James W. Pennebaker and Robin C. O'Heeron, "Confiding in Others and Illness Rate Among Spouses of Suicide and Accidental-Death Victims," *J. of Abnormal Psychology*, Vol. 93, No. 4 (November 1984), 473–476.

7. Osterweis, Solomon and Green, *op. cit.*, 28 and 284.

8. Erich Lindemann, "Grief and Grief Management: Some Reflections," *J. of Pastoral Care*, Vol. 30, No. 3 (September 1976), 198.

9. E. Markusen and R. Fulton, "Childhood Bereavement and Behavior Disorders: A Critical Review," *Omega: Journal of Death and Dying*, 2 (1971), 107–117.

10. Osterweis, Solomon and Green, *op. cit.*, 99–141 and 284–285.

11. Nancy Horowitz, "Adolescent Mourning Reactions to Infant and Fetal Loss," *Social Casework*, Vol. 59, No. 9 (November 1978), 551–559.

11a. For an excellent discussion of healing grief by healing our image of God, see R. Scott Sullender, *Grief and Growth* (Mahwah, N.J.: Paulist Press, 1985), especially Chapters 8 and 9.

12. Michael B. Russell, "Blessed Are Those Who Mourn," *Sojourners* (January 26, 1982), 24–26. Russell distinguishes between individual grief and political grief as follows: "Political grief is caused by systemic loss rather than one-time individual loss. . . . Political grief is characterized by the persistence of the cause of grief. It is as though someone close to you died every day. The appropriate griefwork must not only apply the process of resolving grief to the group of individuals—it must eliminate the persistent cause of the grief. To successfully resolve political grief, political change must accompany the process of griefwork."

13. Joanna Macy, *Despair and Personal Power in the Nuclear Age* (Philadelphia: New Society Publishers, 1983).

14. Harriet Sarnoff Schiff, *The Bereaved Parent* (New York: Penguin Books, 1977), 16.

15. Phoebe Cranor, "Grief and Inner Healing" (Pecos, N.M.: Dove Publications, 1983), Leaflet #12.

16. Lindemann, *op. cit.*, 198–207. For a discussion of shadow grief, see also Larry G. Peppers and Ronald J. Knapp, *Motherhood & Mourning: Perinatal Death* (New York: Praeger, 1980), Chapter 5, "Shadow Grief."

17. Judy Tombrink and James Hoff, "Dealing with Grief: A Growth Experience," videotape produced by Creighton University, Omaha, Nebraska.

18. Elisabeth Kübler-Ross, *On Death and Dying* (New York: Macmillan, 1969). For further help on how to work through grief, cf. R. Scott Sullender, *Grief & Growth* (New York: Paulist Press, 1985).

19. Phyllis Silverman (ed.), *Helping Each Other in Widowhood* (New York: Health Sciences 1974), 9.

## 2. Healing Grief for the One We Miss the Most

1. Elisabeth Kübler-Ross, *On Death and Dying* (New York: Macmillan, 1969).

## 3. Love Is Stronger than Death

1. Richard Kalish and David K. Reynolds, "Phenomenological Reality and Post-Death Contact," *J. for the Scientific Study of Religion*, Vol. 12, No. 2 (June 1973), 209–221.

2. J. Yamimoto, "Cultural Factors in Loneliness, Death and Separation," *Medical Times*, Vol. 98 (1970), 177–83.

3. Andrew Greeley, *Death and Beyond* (Chicago: Thomas More Press, 1976).

4. Karl Rahner and Johannes Metz, *The Courage To Pray* (New York: Crossroad, 1981).

5. Mark Glasswell and Edward Fashole-Luke (eds.), "Ancestor Veneration and the Communion of Saints," *New Testament Christianity for Africa and the World* (London: SPCK, 1974), 209–221. This article speaks of ancestor worship practiced by Africans (actually veneration rather than worship, the author claims) as an expression of their desire to relate in a loving way to their deceased, and it speaks of the Church's need "to give the Communion of Saints the centrality which the soul of Africa craves."

5a. Eighty percent of the New Testament citations of the Old Testament are from the Greek Septuagint rather than the Hebrew Bible. Thus New Testament writers were familiar with the Maccabean tradition of praying for the deceased. Cf. Philip St. Romain, *Catholic Answers to Fundamentalists' Questions* (Liguori, Mo.: Liguori, 1984), 57.

6. P.W. Keppler, *Poor Souls in Purgatory* (St. Louis: Herder, 1927), 17.

7. The Jewish tradition of prayer for the deceased grew as the concept of an eternal gehenna (place of punishment after death, later translated as hell) waned. By the time of Jesus, rabbis were repelled by the eternal hell depicted by apocalyptic literature, such as the

Book of Enoch (164–161 B.C.). Eternal punishment was limited to a very few cases of notorious sin (e.g., adultery). Even the stern Shammaites recognized a group of sinners who would merely suffer temporarily. Rabbi Hillel (60 B.C.–9 A.D.) founded a more lenient school teaching that twelve months was the maximum punishment for all but the most hardened sinners. This one-year limit was generally accepted in the Talmud and midrash. No Jew was thought to be wicked enough for this maximum penalty, so recitation of the Kaddish to free a Jewish soul from gehenna was limited to eleven months. Sinners in gehenna were permitted to rest from their sufferings on the sabbath and were also helped by those praying on earth. "Gehinnon," *The Universal Jewish Encyclopedia* (New York: Ktav, 1969), Vol. 4, 520–21.

8. "Yizkor," *The Universal Jewish Encyclopedia* (New York: Ktav, 1969), Vol. 10, 603–04.

9. "Death," *The Jewish Encyclopedia* (New York: Funk & Wagnalls, 1903), Vol. 4, 486.

9a. When St. Paul spoke of Christians as being "one body in Christ" he was drawing upon this Old Testament idea which modern scholars call "corporate personality." For St. Paul, the center of corporate personality became the personality of Jesus and all who were united with Jesus were also united to each other in "one body." The concept of the communion of saints arose from Paul's understanding that the body of Christ, like the ancient Hebrew social group, included the deceased as well as the living. Cf. H. Wheeler Robinson, *Corporate Personality in Ancient Israel* (Philadelphia: Fortress, 1964), 25–44 and 58.

10. P.W. Keppler, *op. cit.*, 26.

11. H. Leclercq, DACL 1:68–75. Even earlier, in *Acts of Paul and Thecla* (Ch. 29), Thecla prays for a deceased daughter of her hostess.

12. Wilpert, *Die Malereien der Katakomben Roms*, p. 334. Quoted in Keppler, *op. cit.*, 27.

13. John Chrysostom, *I Ad. Cor.*, Hom, XLI, n. 4, P.G., LXI, Col. 361, 362. Cyprian, *Ep. 1, 2*, CSEL, III, 466ff.

14. Tertullian, *De Monag.*, 10:4; *Corp Christ*, 2:1043 and 2:1243.

15. George Maloney, *The Everlasting Now* (Notre Dame: Ave

Maria Press, 1980), 65. This is a good study of current views on heaven, hell and purgatory. See also Robert Ombres, O.P., *Theology of Purgatory* (Butler, Wis.: Clergy Book Service, 1978), 27–53.

16. Eusebius, *Life of Constantine* 4:71, GCS 7:147. The *Canon of Hippolytus*, probably reflecting widespread third century practices, prays for the dead.

17. Joseph Jungmann, *Mass of the Roman Rite* (New York: Benziger Bros., 1959), 441–43.

18. A. Butler, *Lives of the Saints*, Vol. I (New York: Kenedy, 1956).

19. St. Teresa of Avila did not fear following the guidance of the deceased confessor Pedro Alcantara, who in a vision told her not to compromise with the mayor who wanted the new Convent of St. Joseph to be endowed rather than having no income as Teresa preferred. Teresa was ready to give in, but the vision made her stand firm until the mayor gave in. Cf. Mary Donze, *Teresa of Avila* (Ramsey, N.J.: Paulist, 1982). She also saw her benefactor Bernardino d'Mendoza suffering in purgatory and then released at her Mass. Does our fear of spiritualism keep us from seeing what Jesus is telling us through the deceased?

20. P.W. Keppler, *op. cit.*, 89.

21. For a study of the change in tradition on purgatory, cf. Robert Ombres, O.P., *op. cit.*, 66. For how to integrate the new eschatology into prayer, see the fine book by George Maloney, *Death, Where Is Your Sting?* (New York: Alba House, 1984).

22. Walter Abbott, S.J. (ed.), *The Documents of Vatican II* (New York: Guild, 1964), "Dogmatic Constitution on the Church (Lumen Gentium)," 81–84.

22a. Richard McBrien, *Catholicism* (Study Edition) (Minneapolis: Winston, 1981), 1144–45.

23. Many of the mystics saw purgatory as a place of healing (hospital) rather than of punishment (prison). For example, St. Catherine of Genoa saw purgatory as a joyful state freely chosen by a soul to be healed of all that blocks God's love. "There is no joy save that in paradise to be compared to the joy of the souls in purgatory. This joy increases day by day because of the way in which the love of God

corresponds to the soul, since the impediment to that love is worn away daily. This impediment is the rust of sin. As it is consumed, the soul is more and more open to God's love." Cf. George Hughes (trans.), *Catherine of Genoa: Purgation and Purgatory* (Ramsey, N.J.: Paulist, 1979), 72.

24. Raymond Moody, *Life After Life* (Covington, Ga.: Mockingbird, 1975) and *Reflections on Life After Life* (New York: Bantam, 1977), 18–22.

25. John Chrysostom, Hom. 3 in *Ep. ad Phil.*, n. 4.

26. Joseph Jungmann, *op. cit.*, 443.

27. Serge Bulgakov, *The Orthodox Church* (London: Centenary Press, 1935), 208–09. For a beautiful synopsis of the Orthodox belief in praying for the dead, cf. Kallistos Ware, "One Body in Christ: Death and the Communion of Saints," *Sobornost*, Vol. 3, No. 2 (1981), 179–91.

28. John Wesley, "A Second Letter to the Author of 'The Enthusiasm of Methodists and Papists Compared,' " in E.R. Hardy, "The Blessed Dead in Anglican Piety," *Sobornost*, Vol. 3, No. 2 (1981), 166.

29. John Wesley, *ibid.*, with quotation from Wesley, *Works* (1830 ed.), IX.55 and X.9.

30. *The Book of Common Prayer* in the litany after morning prayer for Sunday, Wednesday and Friday still retains the traditional prayer for the dead, "Remember not, O Lord, our offenses nor the offenses of our forefathers; neither take vengeance for our sins; spare us, O Lord, spare thy people whom thou has redeemed with thy Precious Blood."

31. Archbishops' Commission on Christian Doctrine, *Prayer and the Departed* (London: SPCK 1971), 20.

32. Dr. Kenneth McAll, *Healing the Family Tree* (London: Sheldon Press, 1982).

33. Carl Jung, *Psychology and Religion: East and West*, Vol. XI, p. 414, in *The Collected Works of Carl Gustav Jung*, ed. Sir Herbert Read, *et al.*, trans. R.F.C. Hull (Princeton: Princeton Univ. Press, 1967).

34. Personal letter from Dr. Kenneth McAll, August 20, 1984.

35. Fyodor Dostoevsky, *The Brothers Karamozov*, tr. from Rus-

sian by Constance Garnett (Chicago: Encyclopaedia Britannica, 1952), Great Books LII, 26.

## 4. How To Pray for the Deceased

1. Paul Keppler, *The Poor Souls in Purgatory* (St. Louis: Herder, 1927), 148.

2. Dr. Kenneth McAll, *Healing the Family Tree* (London: Sheldon Press, 1982).

## 5. What About Hell? Praying for Great Sinners

1. "On Suicide," *Time* (November 25, 1966), 48–49.

2. *Idem.*

3. Documents #72, 76, 801, 858 and 1306 in Denzinger-Schönmetzer, *Enchiridion Symbolorum, Definitionum et Declarationum* (Freiburg i. B.: Herder, 1963).

3a. Richard McBrien, *op. cit.*, 1152.

4. Joachim Jeremias, *The Proclamation of Jesus* (New York: Charles Scribner's Sons, 1972), 116, 117, describes the parable of the prodigal son in terms of the eschatological meal in which "the endtime brings with it a reversal of conditions. In this reversal, salvation comes to the sinner, not the righteous."

5. Charles H. Giblin, "Structural and Theological Considerations on Lk 15," *Catholic Biblical Quarterly*, Vol. 24 (1962), 16.

6. Joachim Jeremias, *Rediscovering the Parables* (New York: Charles Scribner's Sons, 1966), 107. "The future tense in Lk 15:7 is to be understood as referring to the last days: at the final judgment God will rejoice when among the many righteous he finds a sinner who has repented and on whom he may pronounce absolution—indeed it will give him even greater joy."

7. Kenneth Bailey, *Poet and Peasant* (Grand Rapids: Eerdmans, 1976), 164.

8. *Ibid.*, 179–80.

9. *Ibid.*, 176–77.

10. *Ibid.*, 183–84.

11. *Ibid.*, 195.

12. *Ibid.*, 184–85.

## 6. Praying for the Family Tree

1. A. Nicholas Groth, psychologist and director of the Sex Offenders Program for the Connecticut Department of Corrections, found that eighty-one percent of the sex offenders were exposed to sex victimization as children. *Psychology Today* (May 1984), 44.

2. W. Hugh Missildine, *Your Inner Child of the Past* (New York: Simon & Schuster, 1982).

3. John Howells, *Theory and Practice of Family Psychiatry* (N.Y.: Mazel, 1971), 77–80, 843–863.

4. Ivan Boszormenyi-Nagy and Geraldine Spark, *Invisible Loyalties: Reciprocity in Intergenerational Family Therapy* (N.Y.: Harper & Row, 1973), 97.

5. *Ibid.*, 68.

6. Kenneth McAll, *Healing the Family Tree* (London: Sheldon, 1982).

7. Kenneth McAll, "Ritual Relieved Phantom Pain," *J. of Christian Healing*, Vol. 5, No. 1 (1983), 54.

8. Kenneth McAll, *Healing the Family Tree, op. cit.*, 12–15 and unpublished introduction.

9. William Johnston, *The Mirror Mind: Spirituality and Transformation* (New York: Harper & Row, 1981), 135.

10. Madeleine L'Engle, *A Swiftly Tilting Planet* (New York: Dell, 1979). See also two novels by Charles Williams which present in fictional form the reality of the spiritual world and how it impinges on our world, especially through our ongoing relationship with the deceased: *All Hallow's Eve* (Grand Rapids: Eerdmans, 1948) and *Descent Into Hell* (Grand Rapids: Eerdmans, 1937).

11. Dr. Kurt Koch through dealing with hundreds of occult cases also sees the occult influence as inherited and highly recommends the Eucharist. Cf. Kurt Koch, *Christian Counseling and Occultism* (Grand Rapids: Kregel, 1972), 332.

12. George Ritchie and Elizabeth Sherrill, *Return from Tomorrow* (Grand Rapids: Zondervan, 1983).

## 7. Healing Relationships with Miscarried, Aborted and Stillborn Babies

1. Larry G. Peppers and Ronald J. Knapp, *Motherhood and Mourning* (New York: Praeger, 1980), 14.

2. *1982–83 Statistical Abstract of the U.S.* (Washington, D.C.: Bureau of the Census), 70; National Center for Health Statistics, *Annual Summary of Births, Deaths, Marriages and Divorces, U.S., 1983*, 1 (reports 3,614,000 live births in 1983).

3. Peppers and Knapp, *ibid.*

4. Augustine believed that the judgment scene of Matthew 25 offered only a choice between heaven on the right hand and hell on the left hand. Since the unbaptized could not obtain heaven with their original sin, he had to assign them to hell. "Those unfortunate children who die without baptism must face the judgment of God. They are vessels of contumely, vessels of wrath and the wrath of God is upon them. Baptism is the only thing that can deliver these unfortunate infants from the kingdom of death and the power of the devil. . . . There can be no doubt about the matter: they will go into eternal fire with the devil." Although Augustine eventually revised his opinion, later theologians ignored this. Cf. George Dyer, *Limbo: Unsettled Question* (New York: Sheed & Ward, 1964), 6.

5. Aquinas argued that since original sin is a deprivation of grace, but not an actual personal sin, the unbaptized child is not personally guilty or deserving of punishment. St. Thomas Aquinas, *Commentary on the Sentences*, II, d. 33, q. 2.

6. For a brief summary of the historical evolution of limbo, cf. *Sacramentum Mundi*, "Limbo," Peter Gumpel (New York: Herder & Herder, 1968), III:318. See also Edmund Fortman, *Everlasting Life After Death* (New York: Alba House, 1977), Chapter 7, "Is There a Limbo for Infants?" especially 143–55.

7. "An official endorsement of limbo's existence by the

Church is not to be found." "Limbo," *New Catholic Encyclopedia*, Vol. 8, 762–765. See also Fortman, *op. cit.*, 150.

8. J.T. Ryan interviewing Monika Hellwig, "Life After Death," *Sign* (April 1979), 35.

9. Austin Flannery, O.P. (ed.), *Vatican Council II: The Conciliar and Post-Conciliar Documents*, "The Church," IIa:16; "The Church in the Modern World," Part I, I:22.

10. *New Catholic Encyclopedia*, Vol. 8, 763; Fortman, *op. cit.*, 153. An example of baptism of desire supplied by the family is that of St. Perpetua, who had a vision of her brother Dinocrates, who had died at the age of seven. Dinocrates appeared unable to drink from a fountain, which St. Perpetua took to be the fountain of baptism. She prayed daily for Dinocrates, and then had another vision in which her brother appeared happy, healed of the illness which took his life, and able to drink from the eternal fountain. Cf. E.C.E. Owens, *Some Authentic Acts of the Early Martyrs* (London: SPCK, 1833), 82–84.

11. *Sacramentum Mundi*, *op. cit.*, 318.

12. Fortman, *op. cit.*, 148–49.

13. St. Thomas Aquinas, *Summa Theologica*, II–II, q. 83, a. 5, ad 1.

14. *Omaha World Herald* (November 17, 1982), 1 and 3.

15. "When the Foetus Isn't Listening," *Medical World News*, April 10, 1970, 28–29; A.W. Liley, "The Fetus as a Personality," *Aust. N. Z. J. Psychiatry*, Vol. 6, No. 99 (1972), 99–105; Lester W. Sontag and Robert F. Wallace, "The Movement Response of the Human Fetus to Sound Stimuli," *Child Dev.*, Vol. 6 (1935), 253–58.

16. Liley, *op. cit.*, 102.

17. *Ibid.*, 101–02; E. Blechschmidt, "Human Being from the Very First," in Hilgers, Horan and Mall (eds.), *New Perspectives on Human Abortion* (Frederick, Md.: University Publications of America, 1981), 23; John T. Noonan, Jr., "The Experience of Pain by the Unborn," in Jeff Lane Hensely (ed.), *The Zero People* (Ann Arbor: Servant Books, 1983), 141–56.

18. Chester B. Martin, Jr., "Behavioral States in the Human Fetus," *J. Reprod. Med.*, Vol. 26, No. 8 (August 1981), 425–32; R.S.G.M. Bots, *et al.*, "Human Fetal Eye Movements: Detection in

Utero by Ultrasonography," *Early Human Dev.*, 5 (1981), 87–94; *Modern Medicine* (March 23, 1970), 43.

19. Liley, *op. cit.*, 101.

20. David K. Spelt, "The Conditioning of the Human Fetus in Utero," *J. Experimental Psychology*, Vol. 38, No. 3 (June 1948), 338–46.

21. Frank Lake, *Tight Corners in Pastoral Counseling* (London: Darton, Longman & Todd, 1981), 2 and 36.

22. Quoted in Morton Kelsey, *Afterlife: The Other Side of Dying* (Ramsey, N.J.: Paulist, 1979), 106–07. See also Linda Mathison, "Birth Memories: Does Your Child Remember?" *Mothering* (Fall 1981), 103–07. Mrs. Mathison describes numerous examples of small children who recalled prenatal and birth experiences, without attempting to explain the mechanism for such memories.

23. *Chicago Tribune*, "Embryos Can Remember, Therapist Says" (November 1, 1978); Andrew Feldmar, "The Embryology of Consciousness: What Is a Normal Pregnancy?" in David Mall and Walter Watts (eds.), *The Psychological Aspects of Abortion* (Washington, D.C.: University Publications of America, 1979), 15–24.

24. Frank Lake, *op. cit.*, Chapter 2, "Counseling in the Presence of Primal Pain," 14–37.

25. David B. Cheek, "Maladjustment Patterns Apparently Related to Imprinting at Birth," *Am. J. Clinical Hypnosis*, Vol. 18, No. 2 (October 1975), 75–82; R. Gaddini, "Early States and Neonatal Psychology," in L. Carenza and L. Zichella (eds.), *Emotion and Reproduction* (London: Academic Press, 1979), 1076–78.

26. Robert MacDonald, M.D., *Memory Healing* (Atlanta: RLM Ministries, 1981), 34–36.

27. Antonio J. Ferreira, "Emotional Factors in the Prenatal Environment," *J. Nervous and Mental Disease*, Vol. 141, No. 1 (1965), 112–13; Ashley Montagu, *Life Before Birth* (New York: Signet, 1965), 156–71.

28. Thomas Verny, *Secret Life of the Unborn Child* (New York: Summit, 1981), 87–88.

29. Verny, *op. cit.*, 76.

30. Montagu, *op. cit.*, 152.

31. Lester W. Sontag, "Prenatal Determinants of Postnatal Behavior," in Harry Waisman and George Kerr (eds.), *Fetal Growth and Development* (New York: McGraw-Hill, 1970), 267–68.

32. Dimity B. Carlson and Richard C. Labarba, "Maternal Emotionality During Pregnancy and Reproductive Outcome: A Review of the Literature," *Int. J. Behavioral Dev.*, 2 (1979), 343–76.

33. Lester Sontag, "The Significance of Fetal Environmental Differences," *Am. J. Ob. and Gyn.*, Vol. 42, No. 6 (December 1941), 1000–1002; Carlson and Labarba, *op. cit.*, Antonio J. Ferreira, *op. cit.*, 112; Elizabeth K. Turner, "The Syndrome in the Infant Resulting from Maternal Emotional Tension During Pregnancy," *Med. J. Australia* (February 11, 1956), 221–222.

34. D.H. Stott, "Follow-up Study from Birth of the Effects of Pre-Natal Stresses," *Develop. Med. Child. Neurol.*, 15 (1973), 770–787.

35. Verny, *op. cit.*, 48.

36. Charles Spezzano, "Prenatal Psychology: Pregnant with Questions," *Psychology Today*, May 1981, pp. 49–57. Other researchers have investigated a variety of ways in which prenatal influences may affect later life. Cf. Antonio J. Ferreira, "The Pregnant Woman's Emotional Attitude and Its Reflection on the Newborn," *Am. J. of Orthopsychiatry*, 30 (3), July 1960, pp. 533–561; Sarnoff A. Mednick, "Breakdown in Individuals at High Risk for Schizophrenia: Possible Predispositional Perinatal Factors," *Mental Hygiene*, 54(1), January 1970, pp. 50–63; Sarnoff A. Mednick, "Birth Defects and Schizophrenia," *Psychology Today*, 4(11), April 1971, pp. 48–50, 80–81; Melvin Zax, *et al.*, "Birth Outcomes in the Offspring of Mentally Disordered Women," *Amer. J. Orthopsychiatry*, 47(2), April 1977, pp. 218–30; Alex J. Crandon, "Maternal Anxiety and Obstetric Complications," *J. of Psychosom. Res.*, 23, 1979, pp. 109–11; Matti O. Huttenen and Pekka Niskanen, "Prenatal Loss of Father and Psychiatric Disorder," *Arch. Gen. Psychiatry*, 35, April 1978, pp. 429–431; Lester W. Sontag, "War and the Fetal-Maternal Relationship," *Marriage and Family Living*, 6(1), Winter 1944, pp. 3–4, 16; *Medical World News*, "Prenatal Hormones Change Styles of Play," March 31, 1980, pp. 35–36; Gian-Paolo Ravelli, *et al.*, "Obesity in Young Men After Fa-

mine Exposure in Utero and Early Infancy," *N.E.J. of Med.*, 295(7), August 12, 1976, pp. 349–353.

37. Verny, *op. cit.*, 22–23.

38. Clifford Olds, "Fetal Response to Music," *PPPANA News*, No. 1 (April 1984), 2.

39. Verny, *op. cit.*, 46–49; Francis MacNutt, "Prayers for the Unborn Child," *Charisma* (November 1983), 24 and 28–31.

40. S.N. Bauer, "Science of Touch and Feeling Has Great Import for Preborn," *St. Cloud Visitor*, Vol. 71, No. 24 (November 11, 1982), 1 and 11. See also Conrad W. Baars, M.D., *Feeling and Healing Your Emotions* (Plainfield, N.J.; Bridge, 1979), 81–84.

41. St. Thomas Aquinas, *Summa Theologica*, I–II, q. 81, art. 1 and 2.

42. John and Paula Sandford, *Restoring the Christian Family* (Plainfield, N.J.: Bridge, 1979), 128–29.

43. Metropolitan Anthony of Surozh, "The Suffering and Death of Children," *Eastern Churches Review*, Vol. 8, No. 2 (1976), 110.

44. P.F.H. Giles, "Reactions of Women to Perinatal Death," *Aust. N. Z. J. Obstet. Gynaec.*, 10 (1970), 207–10; Karen Kowalski and Watson A. Bowes, Jr., "Parents' Response to a Stillborn Baby," *Contemporary Ob/Gyn*, 8, (October 1976), 53–57; John Kennell, Howard Slyter and Marshall H. Klaus, "The Mourning Response of Parents to the Death of a Newborn Infant," *N. E. J. Med.*, Vol. 238, No. 7 (August 13, 1970), 344–49.

45. Theresa M. Stephany, "Early Miscarriages: Are We Too Quick To Dismiss the Pain?" *RN Magazine* (November 1982), 89.

46. Larry G. Peppers and Ronald J. Knapp, "Maternal Reactions to Involuntary Fetal-Infant Death," *Psychiatry*, 43 (May 1980), 155–59.

47. Peppers and Knapp, *Motherhood and Mourning, op. cit.*

48. *Ibid.*, 19–22.

49. Jack M. Stack, "Spontaneous Abortion and Grieving," *Am. Family Physician*, Vol. 21, No. 5 (May 1980), 99–102; Robert T. Corney and Frederick T. Horton, Jr., "Pathological Grief Following

Spontaneous Abortion, *Am. J. Psychiatry*, Vol. 131, No. 7 July 1974, 825–29.

50. Marshall H. Klaus and John H. Kennell, *Parent-Infant Bonding* (St. Louis: C.V. Mosby, 1982), 264.

51. Harriet Sarnoff Schiff, *The Bereaved Parent* (New York: Penguin, 1977), 33–35.

52. Kennell and Klaus, *op. cit.*, 265.

53. Schiff, *op. cit.*, 79.

54. *Ibid.*, 90.

55. Peppers and Knapp, *op. cit.*, 29; Elizabeth K. Best, "Grief in Response to Prenatal Loss: An Argument for the Earliest Prenatal Attachment," *Dissertation Abstracts International*, Vol. 42, No. 6 (December 1981); Machelle Seibel and William L. Graves, "The Psychological Implications of Spontaneous Abortion," *J. Reprod. Med.*, Vol. 25, No. 4 (October 1980), 161–65.

56. Terry Selby, M.S.W., "Agonizing Aftermath of Abortion." Address given at Minnesota Citizens Concerned for Life 1984 State Convention. (Tape available from MCCL, 4249 Nicollet Ave., So., Minneapolis, Minn. 55409.)

57. Ian Kent, *et al.*, "Emotional Sequelae of Elective Abortion," *BC Med. J.*, Vol. 20, No. 4 (April 1978), 118–19. See also Ian Kent and William Nicholls, "Bereavement in Post-Abortive Women: A Clinical Report," *World Journal of Psychosynthesis*, Vol. 13, No. 4 (Autumn–Winter 1981), 14–17. (Reprints available from Ian Kent, M.D., 925 W. Georgia St., #1321, Vancouver, B.C., V6C 1R5, Canada.)

58. Jesse O. Cavenar, Allan A. Maltbie and John L. Sullivan, "Aftermath of Abortion: Anniversary Depression and Abdominal Pain," *Bull of the Menninger Clinic*, Vol. 42, No. 5 (1978), 433–38; R.F.R. Gardner, *Abortion: The Personal Dilemma* (Grand Rapids: Eerdmans, 1972), Chapter 23, "Mental and Spiritual Results of Abortion," 201–211; Nadia B. Gould, "Postabortive Depressive Reactions in College Women," *J. of the Am. College Health Assoc*, Vol. 28, No. 6 (June 1980), 316–20; Francis J. Kane, Jr. and John A. Ewing, "Therapeutic Abortion—Quo Vadimus," *Psychosomatics*, 9 (July–August 1968), 202–07; R. Kumar and Kay Robson, "Previous Induced

Abortion and Anti-Natal Depression in Primiparae: Preliminary Report of a Survey of Mental Health in Pregnancy," *Psychological Medicine*, 8 (1978), 711–715; David Mall and Walter F. Watts, *The Psychological Aspects of Abortion, op. cit.*; Myre Sim, "Abortion and the Psychiatrist," *Br Med J*, 2 (July 20, 1963), 145–48; Jean G. Spaulding and Jesse O. Cavenar, Jr., "Psychoses Following Therapeutic Abortion," *Am. J. Psychiatry*, Vol. 135, No. 3 (March 1978), 364–65; Terry Selby, *op. cit.* See also Nancy Buckles, "Abortion: A Technique for Working through Grief," *College Health*, Vol. 30 (February 1982), 181–82. Although the author acknowledges relatively little negative aftereffects of abortion, she does recognize that some women become "stuck" and describes a counseling technique for helping them resolve negative feelings. Her technique includes steps of focusing attention on the aborted child, establishing some positive remembrance of it and then saying goodbye to the child. These steps are strikingly like our own steps of prayer, given in this chapter. The difference is that Ms. Buckles seems to view the child as only a part of the mother's inner world (albeit a part with which she needs to be reconciled) rather than as a separate being with an ongoing existence who needs Jesus' and our healing and reconciling love.

59. Mary Meehan, "Baby Blues," *Catholic Twin Circle* (August 14, 1983), 4; *Christian Life*, Vol. 46, No. 9 (January 1985), 49.

60. Cited in George Maloney, *Death, Where Is Your Sting? op. cit.*, 78.

61. Arthur Kornhaber, "An Emotional History of the Abortions of Three Women," in James T. Burtchaell, *Abortion Parley* (New York: Andrews & McMeel, 1979).

62. For example, Drs. Robert Weil and Carl Tupper studied eighteen women who had had three or more consecutive miscarriages. These women were given weekly psychotherapy during a subsequent pregnancy, and fifteen successfully delivered a child, indicating that therapy for emotional wounds can interrupt a habit of spontaneous abortion. Robert J. Weil and Carl Tupper, "Personality, Life Situation and Communication: A Study of Habitual Abortion," *Psychosom. Med.*, Vol. 22, No. 6 (1960), 448–57. See also Flanders Dunbar, "A Psychosomatic Approach to Abortion and the

Abortion Habit," in Harold Rosen (ed.), *Abortion in America* (Boston: Beacon Press, 1967) 22–31; Dan G. Hertz, "Rejection of Mother-hood," *Psychosomatics*, 14 (July/August 1973), 241–44; L. Kaij, A. Malmquist and A. Nilsson, "Psychiatric Aspects of Spontaneous Abortion—II. The Importance of Bereavement, Attachment and Neurosis in Early Life," *J. Psychosom. Research*, 13 (1969), 53–59; M. Bourgeois and D. Labrousse, "Induced Abortions and Spontaneous Abortions: Psychopathological Aspects Apropos of a Preliminary Sample of 411 Requests for Pregnancy Interruption," *Ann. Med. Psychol.* (Paris), Vol. 2, No. 2 (July 1975), 339–66; Yu-Mei Chao, "An Habitual Aborter's Self-Concept During the Course of a Successful Pregnancy," *Maternal-Child Nursing J.*, Vol. 6, No. 3 (Fall 1977), 165–75.

63. Kent and Nicholls, *op. cit.*: "Further exploration of these feelings in most cases led to the insight that such self-destructive be-havior had come about through (until then unconscious) identifica-tion with the woman's rejecting mother, who had herself unconsciously, or in some cases even consciously, wished to abort her daughter. The latter had introjected these infanticidal wishes of her mother, and had acted them out by identification, in actually suc-ceeding in aborting her own child. Thus, the fetus stood symbolically for herself, while she was identified with the role of her mother. It was noted that a number of the women had had multiple abortions. In view of their level of intelligence and education, and the ready availability of the means of birth control, it must be concluded that they were experiencing a compulsion to become pregnant, setting the stage for the re-enactment of the same identification with their abor-tive mothers. Thus the multiple pregnancies, each leading to an abor-tion, could be interpreted as a form of fractional suicide through the mechanism of identification. Some of these women experienced su-icidal fantasies, or became involved in repeated accidents leading to injury, narrowly escaping death on more than one occasion. While it cannot be claimed that this pattern appeared universally in the cases described, its occurrence was sufficiently well-attested to be signifi-cant, and to alert the psychiatrist to the possibility that such women may be at risk" (15).

64. Terry Selby, *op. cit.*

65. Arthur B. Shostak, Gary McLouth and Lynn Seng, *Men and Abortion* (New York: Praeger, 1984), 16, 40–42, 105–11, 117, 122, 252–53. As sources for the importance of bereavement counseling for men involved in abortion, the authors cite Arthur and Libby Colman, *Earth Father, Sky Father: The Changing Concept of Fathering* (Englewood Cliffs, N.J.: Prentice-Hall, 1981), 128, and counseling psychologist Arnold Medvene, who says that abortion is "undeniably a death experience, a loss experience, and a separation experience with immense reverberations for everybody. If all of that gets blocked and is not resolved, it is bound to have a dramatic and destructive impact on the relationship." See also John Leo, "Sharing the Pain of Abortion," *Time* (September 26, 1983), 78, for a discussion of *Men and Abortion*.

66. Kenneth McAll, *Healing the Family Tree, op. cit.*

67. Personal letter from Dr. Kenneth McAll, August 20, 1984.

68. "Anorexia: The 'Starving Disease' Epidemic," *U.S. News & World Report* (August 30, 1982), 47–48; Cherry Boone O'Neill, *Starving for Attention* (New York: Dell, 1983).

69. Linda Bird Francke, *The Ambivalence of Abortion* (New York: Dell, 1979).

70. Theresa Stephany, *op. cit.*; Cathy C. Floyd, "Pregnancy After Reproductive Failure," *Am. J. of Nursing*, Vol. 81, No. 11 (November 1981), 2050–53; Emanuel Lewis and Ann Page, "Failure To Mourn a Stillbirth: An Overlooked Catastrophe," *Br. J. Med. Psychol.*, 51 (1978), 237–41.

71. Peppers and Knapp, *op. cit.*, 131–35; Floyd, *op. cit.*

72. Albert C. Cain, *et al.*, "Children's Disturbed Reactions to Their Mother's Miscarriage," *Psychosom. Med.*, Vol. 26, No. 1 (1964), 58–66; Kennell and Klaus, *op. cit.*, 276–77; Schiff, *op. cit.*, 83–99; Philip Ney, "A Consideration of Abortion Survivors," in Jeff Lane Hensley (ed.), *The Zero People* (Ann Arbor: Servant, 1983), 123–38.

73. Cain, *et al.*, *op. cit.*, 63; Albert Cain, Irene Fast and Mary Erickson, "Children's Disturbed Reactions to the Death of a Sibling," *Am. J. of Orthopsychiatry*, Vol. 34, No. 4 (July 1964), 741–52.

74. Kennell and Klaus, *op. cit.*, 276–77.

75. *Idem.*; see also Schiff, *op. cit.*, 83–100, where she describes her study of surviving siblings who could recall no positive interaction with their parents during the period after their brother or sister died.

76. For the grief reactions of children at various ages, cf. Judy Tombrink and James Hoff, "Dealing with Grief: A Growth Experience," videotape produced by Creighton University, Omaha, Nebraska.

77. Marian Osterweis, Fredric Solomon and Morris Green (eds.), *Bereavement: Reactions, Consequences, and Care* (Washington, D.C.: National Academy Press, 1984), 99–141 and 284–85. Report of a study by the National Institute of Medicine.

78. *Ibid.*

79. Philip Ney in Hensley, *op. cit.*, 125, gives an account of a patient which is reminiscent of Julie's attachment to her dolls: "A seven-year-old patient reported a dream in which three siblings went with him to play in a sand bank. While playing, the undermined bank collapsed and buried his siblings. Who they were he could not tell me but he knew they were brothers and/or sisters. His mother admitted to three early miscarriages but insisted her child could not have known."

## 8. The Soul Lives Where It Loves

1. Raymond Moody, *Life After Life* (Covington, Ga.: Mockingbird, 1975).

2. Dr. Karlis Osis and Dr. Erlendur Haraldsson, *At the Hour of Death* (New York: Avon, 1977). Cited in Morton Kelsey, *Afterlife: The Other Side of Dying* (New York: Crossroad, 1982), 91–93.

3. "There's a River of Life," words and music by L. Casebolt (Dorset, England: Celebration Services, 1971, 1975).

4. K. R. Hanley, "Reflections on Gabriel Marcel's Theme of Presence as a Sign of Immortality," unpublished English version of an article published in French in the *Revue Philosophique de Louvain*, tome 74, May 1976.

5. George Maloney, *The Everlasting Now* (Notre Dame: Ave Maria, 1980), 98–99.

6. Quoted in George Maloney, *Inward Stillness* (Denville, N.J.: Dimension, 1976), 190–91.

## Conclusion

1. Maurice Zundel, *The Splendor of the Liturgy* (New York: Sheed and Ward, n.d.).

## Appendix A: What About Hell? How Can a Loving God Send Anyone There?

1. Jesus' very mission was to proclaim the end to vindictive punishment. Thus in Luke 4:14–19 Jesus in the Nazareth synagogue proclaims his own mission using the words of Isaiah 61:1–2. But why after proclaiming his mission was the whole audience filled with indignation to the point of wanting to hurl Jesus over the edge of the mountain (Lk 4:30)? The Jewish listeners wanted the Messiah to be vengeful to the Romans, to the Sidonians, to the Syrians—to all but themselves. But Jesus skipped the sentence in Isaiah 61:2 which spoke of God's vengeance on enemies and instead declared that God's "favor" rested on all, Romans, Sidonians and Syrians alike (Lk 4:26–27). Jesus angered the Jewish listeners because he was proclaiming the end of vengeful punishments and the reign of a Messiah whose "favor" shines on the just and the unjust. As Robert Jewett explains, by skipping the sentence regarding God's vengeance and thus placing himself in opposition to the vengeance tradition, Jesus violates the literal interpretation of Scripture prevalent in his time and thus places himself in mortal danger. Robert Jewett, *Jesus Against the Rapture* (Phildelphia: Westminster Press, 1979), 51–65.

2. Kenneth Bailey, *Poet and Peasant, op. cit.*, 195.

3. *Ibid.*, 195–96.

4. Cited by George Maloney, *The Everlasting Now* (Notre Dame: Ave Maria, 1980), 121.

5. William J. Dalton, S.J. *Salvation and Damnation* (Theology Today Series, #41; Butler, Wis.: Clergy Book Service, 1977), especially pp. 69–73 and 83. Dalton argues that while an eternal hell is

an *abstract* possibility, given what we know of the loving nature of God we may have real hope that he will actually save all.

6.  Piet Schoonenberg, S.J., "I Believe in Eternal Life," *Concilium, Dogma, the Problem of Eschatology* (New York: Herder & Herder, 1969), 110.

7.  George Maloney, S.J., *Inward Stillness* (Denville, N.J.: Dimension, 1976), 194.

8.  Kenneth Bailey, *The Cross and the Prodigal* (St. Louis: Concordia, 1973), 126–30.

9.  John A.T. Robinson, *In the End God* (New York: Harper & Row, 1968), 133.

10.  Matthew & Dennis Linn, S.J., *Deliverance Prayer* (Ramsey, N.J.: Paulist Press, 1980). Collection of essays discussing deliverance prayer from experiential, psychological and theological perspectives.

11.  Karl Rahner and other theologians suggest that what the Church needs today is a reformulation of Church dogma concerning hell. K. Rahner, "The Hermeneutics of Eschatological Assertions," in *Theological Investigations*, Vol. IV (Baltimore: Helicon, 1966). This reformulation of dogma is especially critical because many of the official statements of the teaching Church are based on the literal interpretations of such scriptual words as "fire," "everlasting," and "hell," whereas Jesus intended a symbolic interpretation. Dalton gives the following example: "In the first Ecumenical Council of Lyons we are required to believe that the damned 'are forever tortured in the fires of everlasting gehenna' (Dz 839). Whatever the fathers of the council thought, their words today are misleading, even erroneous, if they are not interpreted symbolically." Dalton, *op. cit.*, 80.

12.  For Jewish understanding of prayer for the deceased, see Chapter 3, footnote 7 of this book.

13.  *Aiónios* is an adjective formed from the Greek noun *aión* which the *Greek-English Lexicon of the New Testament* lists as meaning an indefinite period of time ranging from a "generation" or a man's "lifetime" to "lasting forever." Scripture scholar Wm. Barclay in commenting on those meanings says, "We shall never enter into the full ideas of eternal life until we rid ourselves of the almost instinctive assumption that eternal life means primarily life which goes on for-

ever." Barclay further comments, "The essence of the word *aiónios* is that it is the word of the eternal order as contrasted with the order of this world; it is the word of deity as contrasted with humanity; essentially it is the word which can be properly applied to no one other than God. *Aiónios* is the word which describes nothing less and nothing other than the life of God." Wm. Barclay, *New Testament Words* (Philadelphia: Westminster Press, 1974), 33–41.

14. George Maloney, *The Everlasting Now, op. cit.*, 111.

15. When Jesus speaks about gehenna or hell, he uses contemporary images (e.g., God sending people there, everlasting punishment or even total annihilation) without judging their theological accuracy. He does not discuss such questions as intercession for the condemned souls or a twelve month time limit on all but the most wicked, because he is not trying to describe accurately a place of future punishment. Rather, as in other places where Jesus speaks about the threat of vindictive punishment, he is not speaking because he intends to send people to hell, but rather to show how important it is to obey so that his disciples can love each other more. Thus, for instance, in Matthew 25 he uses such imagery to underline his deep ultimate concern for human values like feeding the hungry, clothing the naked and visiting those in prison. Because Jesus' apocalyptic images are meant to accurately underline his deep ultimate concern for his followers to love one another, rather than meant to accurately describe future punishment, "the metaphors in which Jesus describes the eternal perdition of man as a possibility which threatens him at this moment are images (fire, worm, darkness) taken from the mental furniture of contemporary apocalyptic literature . . . Even such a term as 'eternal loss' is in the nature of an image." Karl Rahner, "Hell" in *Sacramentum Mundi* (New York: Herder & Herder, 1969), 7–8; "Gehinnom," in *The Universal Jewish Encyclopedia*, Vol. 4 (New York: Ktav, 1969), 520–21; J.L. McKenzie, *Dictionary of the Bible* (Milwaukee: Bruce, 1965), 300, 801; see also Dalton, *op. cit.*, 17–73 for a discussion of images of hell in Scripture.

16. Kallistos Ware, " 'One Body in Christ': Death and the Communion of Saints," *Sobornost*, Vol. 3, No. 2 (1981), 184.

17. #858 and #1002 in a collection of Church documents, Den-

zinger-Schönmetzer, *Enchiridion Symbolorum, Definitionum et Declarationum* (Freiburg i.B. Herder, 1963).

18. George Maloney, *The Everlasting Now, op. cit.*, 77–78. See also Serge Bulgakov, *The Orthodox Church* (London: Centenary Press, 1935), 208–09.

19. Robinson, *op. cit.*, 44.

20. Raymond Moody, *Life After Life* (Covington, Ga.: Mockingbird, 1975). See also Moody, *Reflections on Life After Life* (New York: Bantam, 1977).

21. Survey of literature on near-death experiences by John Heaney, S.J., *The Sacred and the Psychic* (Ramsey, N.J.: Paulist Press, 1984), 139.

22. Plowboy, "The Plowboy Interview: Elisabeth Kübler-Ross on Living, Dying . . . and Beyond," *The Mother Earth News*, May–June 1983.

23. Maurice Rawlings, M.D., *Beyond Death's Door* (New York: Nelson, 1978).

24. Kenneth Ring, *Life at Death; A Scientific Investigation of Near-Death Experience* (New York: Coward, McCann & Geoghegan, 1980).

25. For a review of studies of near-death experiences and their theological significance, see John Heaney, S.J., *op. cit.*, Chapter 8, "Recent Studies of Near-Death Experiences," 129–48. Heaney concludes that the near-death experience may be a literal experience of the next world or an archetypal symbolic experience not of the person's own world. But even if the near-death experience is purely a subjective, archetypal experience, it is a healing experience.

### Appendix B: Non-Catholic Support
### for Praying for the Departed

1. Archbishops' Commission on Christian Doctrine, *Prayer and the Departed* (London: SPCK, 1971), 20.

2. Douglas W. Schoeninger, "Thoughts on Praying for Departed 'Loved Ones,'" *Journal of Christian Healing*, Vol. 6, No. 1 (1984), 53–54.

3. United Synagogue of America, *High Holy Day Prayer Book*

(Bridgeport, Conn.: Prayer Book Press of Media Judaica, Inc., 1951), 327.

## Appendix C: Praying for Family Occult Involvement

1. C.S. Lewis, *The Screwtape Letters* (New York: Macmillan, 1961).

2. Kenneth McAll, *Healing the Family Tree, op. cit.*, 70–71.

3. Curses are often placed on a person three times in mockery of the Trinity. Such curses and occult bondage can be broken by receiving the Eucharist and saying three times, "In the name of Jesus Christ I renounce all occult practices and break all occult bondage of my own or of my forefathers, especially (name any known occult bondage and practices), and I give myself totally to Jesus forever."

4. Both Dr. Kurt Koch and Dr. Kenneth McAll recommend release from the occult influence through the processes of "accurate diagnosis, renunciation, confession of sin and its absolution, prayer of command, and the building up of life with the help of a loving community involved with God's word, prayer and especially the Eucharist." Kenneth McAll, *op. cit.*, 77.

5. Dennis and Matthew Linn (eds)., *Deliverance Prayer* (Ramsey, N.J.: Paulist Press, 1981).

## Appendix D: Blessing Places

1. Kenneth McAll, *Healing the Family Tree, op. cit.*, 61.

2. *The Roman Ritual* (Milwaukee: Bruce Publishing Co., 1964).

# Pamphlets Based on
## *Healing the Greatest Hurt*

**"Prayer for the Dead that Heals the Living."** Based on the first part of chapter 4 of this book, this leaflet is ideal for ministering to those who are mourning for a loved one. It outlines three steps that can bring comfort and hope to all. It is an excellent resource for wake services, counseling sessions, and home visits.

**"Healing Relationships with Miscarried, Aborted and Stillborn Babies."** Condensed from chapter 7 of this book, the leaflet explains the need for healing both the unborn and the living in cases of miscarriage, abortion and stillbirth. It concludes with a parents' prayer for such a child. This leaflet will be helpful to all who minister in hospitals or work with parents after such traumatic experiences.

**"At Peace with the Unborn: A Book for Healing."** This 48 page booklet is a reprint of chapter 7 of this book. Like the leaflet above, it will be helpful to those involved in ministry to parents after the loss of an unborn child.

### Audio and Video Cassettes for
*Healing the Greatest Hurt Retreat*

This retreat focuses on healing the loss of our loved ones.

**Audio and Video Cassettes:** The conferences which are based on this book are available in either audio or video cassette. These conferences invite the retreatant to experience the healing power of praying alone or with another when grieving a death.

Previously available as Theme 3 of *Praying with Another for Healing*, these four half hour conferences are now available on one video cassette. Three of these sessions are also available on one 90 minute audio cassette.

**Retreat Guide:** Theme 3 of *Praying with Another for Healing* suggests follow-up exercises for those wishing a more in-depth prayer experience or seeking to share this retreat with others.

These cassettes may be rented on a donation basis or purchased by completing the order form below.

**Rental Requests:**   Christian Video Library
4453 McPherson
St. Louis, MO 63108
(314) 531-6351

## ORDER FORM

**SHIP AND BILL TO:**

NAME_____

INSTITUTION_____

STREET_____

CITY/STATE_____ ZIP_____

TELEPHONE NO._____

☐ I've enclosed a check or money order for
$_____

Please charge the following credit card
☐ Master Card  ☐ VISA
Minimum Credit Card Order $10.00
Fill in credit card account number below

_____

Expiration
Date_____ DATE_____

SIGNATURE_____

| Format VHS | Beta II | Quantity | Video Cassette Title | Price Each | Total Price |
|---|---|---|---|---|---|
| | | | Healing the Greatest Hurt<br>Video Cassette and Retreat Guide | $99 | |
| | | | Postage and handling:<br>Add $3.50 for Orders under $100;<br>$4.50 for orders from $100–$200;<br>$5.50 for orders from $201–$400. | | |
| | | | **Title of Book/Product** | | |
| | | | Healing the Greatest Hurt<br>Audio Cassette | $6.00 | |
| | | | Retreat Guide (Praying with Another for Healing) | $4.95 | |
| | | | Prayer for the Dead that Heals the Living (pack of 50 leaflets) | $3.00 net | |
| | | | Healing Relationships with Miscarried, Aborted and Stillborn Babies (pack of 50 leaflets) | $3.00 net | |
| | | | At Peace with the Unborn:<br>A Book for Healing | $1.50 | |
| | | | Postage and handling add $1.00 for first $10.00 plus 50¢ for each additional $10.00 ordered | | |
| | | | Total Amount of Check or Money Order | | |